A Woman's Trip to Alaska

1	2	3

1
2
3

1	2	3
4	5	6

FACADE OF

MUIR GLACIER, ALASKA.

A WOMAN'S TRIP TO
ALASKA

BEING AN ACCOUNT OF
A VOYAGE THROUGH THE
INLAND SEAS OF THE
SITKAN ARCHIPELAGO IN
1890

BY

SEPTIMA M. COLLIS
(MRS. GENERAL C. H. T. COLLIS)
AUTHOR OF "A WOMAN'S WAR RECORD."

ILLUSTRATED BY AMERICAN BANK NOTE CO. NEW YORK.

NEW YORK
CASSELL PUBLISHING COMPANY
104 & 106 FOURTH AVENUE

PREFACE.

In the following pages I have not made even a pretence of writing a scientific or historical work. It is not of special interest to those for whom I write to know the exact pressure to the square inch which propels the seas of ice as they furrow their way from the Arctic regions through the mountain gorges down to the softening influences of the Japanese stream, nor to trace the vicissitudes of Alaska from the voyages of Captain Cook down to the purchase by Mr. Seward in 1867, nor yet to familiarize themselves with the ethnology of the various tribes of Indians who inhabit the Aleutian Islands. All this has been better done than I could ever hope to do it. My sole object is to put on paper, for the benefit of others, the impressions made upon me by the voyage, and to explain how this delightful excursion can be enjoyed without the slightest fatigue or discomfort, and at a trifling expense. I want them to know, as I know, that the ship is a yacht, of which the Captain is the host, the passengers his guests, and the object of the cruise the pursuit of pleasure; and if I succeed in inducing my countrywomen to follow my example and postpone Paris and London, Rome and Vienna, the Rhine and the Alps, to some future day, they will always have reason to be grateful to me, and I shall always have reason to be satisfied with my effort.

SEPTIMA M. COLLIS.

No. 75 West 71st Street,
New York, Nov. 7th, 1890.

Mrs. General Collis,
New York City.

Dear Madam:

It was a handsome compliment for you to submit to me the proofs of your forth-coming book "A Woman's Trip to Alaska," every word of which I have read with profit and pleasure, and I am sure it will influence thousands of tourists to visit our own sublime regions in America before going to Europe.

I profess to be somewhat familiar with every route of travel between New York, Puget Sound and British Columbia, and can verify your faithful description as far as Queen Charlotte Sound. Thence to Sitka, Muir Glacier and Juneau, your trip went beyond my personal experience; although I have conversed with many officers who have been there and beyond, all of whom will bear testimony to your faithful descriptions.

In reading your text I was impressed by your appreciation of the heroic achievements of our American pioneers who have brought the Pacific States within easy reach of the most delicate and refined of our Eastern people; that you describe the comfort and real luxury of travel in that new region; the excellent hotels and steamers equal, if not superior, to those of the Atlantic Coast, and the charities of our wealthy to save what is possible of the natives of our newly acquired territory, especially that of Mrs. Elliott F. Shepard, grand-daughter of Commodore Vanderbilt, at Sitka.

I am sure this book will have a large circulation, that it will do much good, and will remain to you and your children a monument more lasting than marble or bronze.

Affectionately your friend,

WM. T. SHERMAN,
General.

CONTENTS.

CHAPTER I.

How to Dress and What to Take.—Checking Baggage.—Trip over the Pennsylvania Railroad.—A Halt and a Dinner in Chicago.—Minneapolis: its Flour-Mills, and its Beautiful Buildings, Lakes, and Parks 1–9

CHAPER II.

West from Minneapolis.—Comforts of the Dining-Car.—Bismarck.—Previous Visit in 1883.—Grant, Villard, and Evarts.—Sitting Bull's Unpopularity.—The Bad Lands.—Marquis de Mores's Unsuccessful Venture.—The Yellowstone River.—Indians, Cowboys, and Ever-changing Scenery.—The Wonders of the Yellowstone Park.—A Trip through it with President Arthur, General Sheridan, and Others, All Now Deceased.—Helena, Montana.—A Sunday Dinner on Board the Train.—Wonderful Trestles and Engineering.—Clark's Fork.—Lake Pend d'Oreille.—The Sportsman's Paradise.—Spokane Falls.—Miles of Uninteresting Sage Grass.—Moxie Farm.—An Amusing Visitor.—The Cascade Mountains.—Stampede Tunnel.—The Puyallup Valley.—Arrival at Tacoma 10–33

CHAPTER III.

Tacoma of Seven Years Ago.—Tacoma of To-Day.—Its Prosperous Population.—Culture and Refinement.—Lumber Mills and Shipping.—Rapid Building.—" The Tacoma" Hotel.—Mount Tacoma, 34–44

CHAPTER IV.

The Steamship *Queen*.—Her Admirable Appointments.—Obliging Officers and Servants.—Captain Carroll and One of his Jokes.—Seattle.—Its Wonderful Growth since the Great Fire.—An Indian's Floating Residence.—Puget Sound.—Its Beautiful Islands.—Wonderful Young Cities.—Anacortes and Fairhaven.—Port Townsend.—Fresh Arrivals from San Francisco 45–56

CONTENTS.

CHAPTER V.

PAGE

Arrival at Victoria, B. C.—An Eden of Flowers.—The English May-
flower.—Exquisite Landscape.—Superb View of the Bay and Mountain Ranges.—Grand Sunset.—Civility of the Residents.—Dinner at
the "Poodle Dog."—A Moonlight Tramp to the Ship . . . 57–66

CHAPTER VI.

Up Early and on Deck.—Who Are the Early Risers?—The Gulf of
Georgia and Johnstone Straits.—Vancouver and San Juan Islands.
—Snow-Clad Mountains.—More Picturesque Islands.—Breakfast.—
Whales, Water-falls, Seals, and Porpoises.—A Most Enjoyable Day.
—Wonderfully Transparent Water. 67–75

CHAPTER VII.

Arrival at Fort Wrangell.—Its History.—Meeting the Governor of
Alaska.—The Totem Poles.—Their Meaning.—Curious Carvings
by the Natives.—The Wretched Indian Homes.—Poverty, Filth, and
Disease.—An Indian Woman's Life of Toil and Shame.—Infanti-
cide.—Polygamy.—Indian Graves.—An Amphibious Hotel.—The
Trip from Fort Wrangell to Sitka.—The Delta of the Stickeen River
—Exquisite Scenery and Long-Continued Daylight.—Arrival at
Sitka 76–88

CHAPTER VIII.

Sitka.—So Much like Naples.—Mt. Edgecombe.—The Dilapidated Store-
Houses.—Baranoff Castle: its History and Reminiscences.—Lady
Franklin and William H. Seward.—The Ceremony of Handing
over Alaska by Russia to the United States.—The Journey of
Civilization Westward around the Globe.—Indians and their Knick-
Knacks.—Superstition against Photography.—Indian Adornments.
—The Rancherie and its Horrors.—Princess Thom.—The American
Shops.—The Russo-Greek Church.—Service by Archbishop Vla-
dimir.—Wonderful Interior Decorations.—American Ladies at
Sitka and How They Live.—The Indian River Walk.—The Blarney
Stone.—Presbyterian Missions and Mrs. Elliott F. Shepard's
Schools and Hospitals.—Wonderful Work of the Missionaries and
Progress of the Pupils.—The Narrow Gulf between Barbarism and
Civilization 89–124

CONTENTS.

CHAPTER IX.

PAGE

Departure from Sitka.—Everybody Happy.—Thoroughly Satisfied with the Day's Experience.—Suggestions for Improvement of Condition of the Sitkans.—The Thousand Islands and their Foliage.—Mt. Edgecombe Again.—The Fairweather Mountains by Twilight.—A Night of Continuous Day.—Amazing Effect of Sunset and Sunrise.—The Dawn of the Morning Finds Everybody on Deck.—Fields of Ice and Icebergs in Glacier Bay.—The Captain's Anxiety and Skill.—"Coffee?" "No, Thanks."—Description of Muir Glacier   . 128–143

CHAPTER X.

My First Sight of Muir Glacier.—The Spell-Bound Passengers.—What it Looks like.—Its Colossal Grandeur and Exquisite Coloring.—Breaking off of the Front with Loud Detonations.—Impressions Made upon Previous Writers.—Ascent to the Top of the Glacier.—Its Dangers and Fatigues   144–158

CHAPTER XI.

Taking Ice Aboard.—The Lake of the Gods and Seidmore Island.—The Fairweathers by Daylight ; Fairweather, Crillon, and La Perouse.—Divine Service on the *Queen*.—Meeting the *Pinta* and Handing the Sailors their Mail.—Douglass Island and its Gold Mines.—History of the Treadwell Mine.—Cheap and Profitable Mining.—A Quarry of Gold.—Juneau.—Prettily Located.—Its History.—Great Depot for Furs.—Methods of the Indian Trader.—A Treasure Lost and Regained.—The Native Dances Given by an Alaskan Showman.—Weird and Unique Performance.—Remarkable Costumes of the Dancers.—The Shaman Dance   159–174

CHAPTER XII.

Taku Inlet.—Up the Lynn Canal to Chilcat, above the 59th Degree of Latitude.—Auk and Eagle Glaciers.—The Davidson Glacier.—Killisnoo and its Fisheries.—Wrangell Narrows and Clarence Straits.—The American Eagle.—Whale Food.—The Oulikon or Candle-Fish.—Schools of Whales in Search of Food.—Bate Inlet.—Fort Simpson, B. C.—A Post of the Hudson Bay Company.—Methodist Church.—Ravages of La Grippe.—Mourning and Tombstones.—"Muck a muck."—The Man-Eaters and Dog-Eaters.—Horrible Barbarism before the Arrival of Mr. William Duncan and the Missionaries.—Death in a Hut, and the Anguish of an Old Squaw   . 175–185

CONTENTS.

CHAPTER XIII.

PAGE

Metlahkatlah, B. C.—An Indian Village with a Good Government.—Their Written Constitution.—Their Industries and Mechanical Education.—Nanaimo.—A Game of Base-Ball.—Celebrated Coal Mines.—Recent Sad Calamity in One of Them.—Great Resort for Sportsmen.—Splendid Fishing and Hunting.—Victoria Again, and the "Poodle Dog" Once More.—'Squimault and the Boating-Grounds.—Election-Day.—The Australian Ballot.—A *Cause Célèbre*.—Arrival Once More at Tacoma.—Off for the Yosemite . . 186–194

ILLUSTRATIONS

By the American Bank Note Company, of New York.

	PAGE
THE MUIR GLACIER—Frontispiece,	
PORTRAIT OF THE AUTHOR—Guttekunst, Phila.	
HOME OF HON. W. D. WASHBURN, MINNEAPOLIS,	7
INDIAN OF THE PLAINS—Photo. by Notman & Son,	9
GEN'L GRANT AT BISMARCK,	13
A BRIEF HALT,	14
HOME OF THE MARQUIS DE MORES,	17
INDIANS AND COWBOYS,	18
OLD FAITHFUL—Photo. by Haynes,	19
YELLOWSTONE FALLS—Photo. by Haynes,	20
PRESIDENT ARTHUR AND COMPANIONS,	21
MARENT TRESTLE—Photo. by Haynes,	24
NEAR CLARK'S FORK—Photo. by Haynes,	25
SPOKANE FALLS—Photo. by Haynes,	27
"AH, THERE!"	30
CUTTING TIMBER IN WASHINGTON—Photo. by Davidson,	32
THE WHARVES AT TACOMA—Photo. by Davidson,	33
TACOMA—Photo. by Rutter,	35
PACIFIC AVENUE, TACOMA—Photo. by Haynes,	38
MOUNT TACOMA—Photo. by Rutter,	42
PUYALLUP HOP-PICKERS,	44
"GIVE HER A COAT OF PAINT,"	48
SEATTLE—Photo. by Haynes,	50
BISHOP VLADIMIR,	55
A BIT OF SCENERY FROM THE DECK,	56
VICTORIA—Photo. by Maynard,	59

	PAGE
VICTORIA HOSPITALITY,	62
ALL HANDS ON DECK,	68
SCENERY IN THE GULF OF GEORGIA,	70
" " " "	70
" " " "	70
" " " "	72
JOHNSTONE STRAITS,	75
FORT WRANGELL,	76
TOTEM POLES AT FORT WRANGELL—Photo. by Taber,	77
A STREET IN FORT WRANGELL—Photo. by Taber,	78
TOTEM POLES AT FORT WRANGELL—Photo. by Taber,	79
INDIAN SQUAWS AT FORT WRANGELL,	81
INDIAN GRAVE AT FORT WRANGELL—from Photo. by Taber,	83
THE STICKEEN DELTA,	85
THE KODAK FIENDS,	86
SITKA (FROM THE WHARF),	88
SITKA (FROM THE BAY)—Photo. by Taber,	91
PORTRAIT OF WILLIAM H. SEWARD,	94
LINCOLN STREET, SITKA—Photo. by Taber,	96
GROUP OF INDIANS AT SITKA,	97
" " " "	99
" " " "	100
" " " "	101
THE RANCHERIE AT SITKA—Photo. by Taber,	102
GROUP OF INDIANS AT SITKA,	103
THE RANCHERIE AT SITKA,	104
PRINCESS THOM,	105
GROUP OF INDIANS AT SITKA,	106
INTERIOR OF INDIAN'S HOUSE AT SITKA—Photo. by Partridge,	107
GREEK CHURCH AT SITKA,	110
INTERIOR OF GREEK CHURCH—Photo. by Alberstone,	113
THE INDIAN RIVER AT SITKA—Photo. by Winter,	117
GROUP OF INDIAN BOYS—Photo. by Winter,	118
MRS. SHEPARD'S TRAINING SCHOOL,	120
THE MISSION CHILDREN,	121
THE MUSEUM AT SITKA,	124
MISSION CHILDREN AND BAND,	125

		PAGE
ON DECK: LEAVING SITKA,		126
A NIGHT OF CONTINUAL DAY,		129
ICEBERGS AHEAD,		131
IN A SEA OF ICE,		132
IMMENSE FLOATING ICE,		135
MUIR GLACIER AT A DISTANCE,		145
A BIT OF THE MUIR GLACIER,		146
THE CLIMB,		153
THE TOP OF MUIR GLACIER—Photo. by Partridge,		156
ON TOP,		157
CANOE RACE BY ALASKA INDIANS,		158
HOISTING ICE ON BOARD,		159
THE TREADWELL GOLD MINES,		162
A WHOLE QUARRY OF GOLD,		163
JUNEAU—Photo. by Taber,		165
ALASKA CURIOS,		168
INDIAN DANCES,		172
INDIAN CANOE,		174
INDIAN WITH THLINKET BLANKET,		174
DAVIDSON GLACIER—Photo. by Winter,		177
KILLISNOO—Photo. by Winter,		178
THE MT. ST. ELIAS RANGE,		180
A PICTURE OF DESPAIR,		185
EDUCATED ALASKA INDIANS AT HOME,		189
THE BOATING GROUNDS AT VICTORIA—Photo. by Maynard,		191
MAP SHOWING ROUTE OF THE STEAMER "QUEEN,"		3d page cover

MY DEAR AMELIA:

To visit Alaska! This, as you know, had been a dream of many years. I had listened enviously to those who had been there; I had read every thing within reach which had been written about it; the more I heard and the more I read, the more I hoped.

At last, most unexpectedly, just as I had completed my arrangements to spend my summer as usual at Saratoga, the welcome words came from your father: "I will have to start for Tacoma in a few days; come along, and run up to Alaska." I don't think I slept any more quietly or soundly that night than did your little one when he hung up his stocking on Christmas eve. Oh, no! Womanlike, I was mentally packing my trunk for the next few hours with the many things which I felt sure would be indispensable to my comfort, and having filled one in the usual style to such an extent that the horrid thing wouldn't shut, I began to ask myself how little would be needed by your father, and whether he couldn't find room for a dress or two in his.

I am not going to tell you what a blunder I made when I really did lay out my stores for the campaign, but I am going to do my best to prevent you following so bad an example, if I can induce you to make the trip.

Dress yourself at the start in a sensible, inexpensive cloth travelling suit, of ordinary warmth; let it fit comfortably and not fashionably (you know what I mean). In addition, carry one, and only one, costume which will serve for church, dinner, theatre, or occasion of ceremony, for I assure you there are two or three places *en route* where the refinements and conventionalities of life are strictly observed, and as you are a fair specimen of your sex, you will want to look up to the standard; otherwise you will feel ill at ease. Of course you will take a proper supply of warm under-garments, and then be sure to add, if they are not already in your portmanteau, the following indispensables: A long fur-lined cloak and an ulster (not a heavy one), which can be put on in a hurry and made to counterfeit an entire costume; otherwise you will be very apt to miss exquisite bits of the ever-changing scenery, because you "are just lying down for a nap and are really not fit to be seen" when some kind friend calls you to run across to the starboard side to see a thousand feet of cascade, visible only for a few minutes, as the boat speeds past it. A warm muff: you will find lots of muffs on the ship, no doubt, but they all keep their hands in their trousers' pockets, and you will sometimes wish you had pockets, too, unless you wrap your little fingers as I suggest. I would several times have given half the money your father had in his purse if I had not left my little seal-skin muff in the camphor closet at home. A pair of broad-soled, low-heeled shoes that have been already worn, with a few nails in sole and heel protruding just enough to impress the smooth surface of the glacial ice. A light-weight mackintosh, with hood. A pair of smoked glasses. A pair of powerful field-glasses. Do all this and you are fully equipped for the journey. Any thing else you take is simply *impedimenta*. As my journey from the Atlantic to the Pacific was so thoroughly enjoyable and restful that I was really loth to leave the train when I reached Tacoma, I cannot better guide you than by telling the story of my own journey.

Having procured our tickets over the Pennsylvania Railroad to Chicago, and thence over the Northern Pacific to Tacoma, we next secured a drawing-room on the Pullman car to Chicago, and telegraphed to that city to secure one to Minneapolis (where we intended to remain over one day). We next had our two trunks taken from our house at Eighty-sixth Street and Fifth Avenue the day before we started and checked through to Minneapolis by the Pennsylvania Railroad Company for fifty cents each; which, I think, was the greatest amount of comfort and relief from anxiety that I ever purchased for a dollar in my life, especially when I found them safely awaiting our coming in that city, ready to be checked through to Tacoma at no additional cost. (In fact I subsequently learned that they could have been checked through the whole distance from my residence to Puget Sound for half a dollar each, if I had so desired.)

At 2 P.M., May 13, 1890, I find myself in the train at Jersey City, westward bound for our destination— Alaska. At Philadelphia we wait five minutes, where you meet me for good-bye and *bon voyage*, to say nothing about a delicious box of bon-bons, and then I settle down to make myself comfortable for the first day's journey. We have a charming little compartment, one of those Pullman *multum-in-parvo*'s which American ingenuity and good taste have contrived to make a long journey a hope instead of a fear; a parlor and dressing-room, where we lounge peacefully and enjoyably with our books and our newspapers. I am, of course, immensely absorbed in reading up the latest authorities on Alaska, my land of years of promise and hope, and, now that my dream is being realized, I proceed to delve into the most recent literature upon the subject. Though darkness came much quicker than it was welcome, still we had an opportunity by daylight of admiring the beautiful valleys and hillsides of Lancaster County, Pennsylvania, all dressed in their spring attire, and although we lost a view of poor Johnstown and the "Horseshoe" on the Alleghanies, yet next day until five o'clock, when we reached Chicago, there was a constant variety of interesting landscape, which was most enjoyable, though there was little of it which lingered in my memory in the august presence of nature's wonders in Alaska. A five-hours' break at Chicago afforded us an opportunity to freshen up and get a good dinner at the Richelieu, a capital hotel, nicely situate on Lake Michigan, where, during my meal, a couple of my *nouveaux-riches* countrymen, who in England would be called "cads," unintentionally afforded me a great deal of fun. One of them who wore a dress-suit, a diamond shirt-stud, and a watch-chain of most attractive proportions, insisted that he must have a *garçon* who spoke French, and this article being supplied, he commenced discussing the *menu* in the very worst French I ever heard, and in so loud a voice that he impressed those who did not know better, that he was some remarkable personage; when, however, he selected the vintage and brand of his *rouge vin* as he called it, I am afraid my outbreak of merriment was observed; it certainly was by the waiter, who felt at once relieved of the high strain of dignified reserve to which he had nerved himself, and fairly guffawed. But the climax came when, in the midst of the meal, another waiter entered and grasped our *distingué* stranger by the hand, with a "Say, when did you get back?" from which I presumed that our Franco-maniac had just returned from a European "tower." I regret to say that from that moment the dialogue of *les deux amis* was continued in home-spun English of a quality as inferior as the French, but the criticism of the viands, and the elevation of the bordeaux to the

electric light to test its color, were maintained to the
end of the feast; yet I think my broiled chicken and
Milwaukee beer (vintage of 1890) were fully as well
appreciated. The whole thing brought vividly to my
mind Mrs. William Florence in one of those inimitable
characters in which she constantly apologizes for her
inability to suppress the impulse to frenchify, as, for
instance, "Now, my dear, *s'asseoir* right here; excuse
my French, but you know I've lived so long abroad."
Perhaps I ought not to refer to such trifles; yet they
are the incidents which will be met with on a trip of
this character, and serve to illustrate the different
phases of American life.

Leaving Chicago at 10 P.M., May 14th, we arrived in
Minneapolis at four next afternoon, and stopped at the
West House, a really superb hotel, unexcelled anywhere I have ever been. I don't know whether to
commend most the amiable and painstaking host, the
excellent, spacious, and well-furnished rooms, capital
laundry, or the admirable arrangement of the ro-
tunda, with its beautiful galleries, where the women
walk or sit after dinner, gazing down at their liege
lords below, swopping wheat and stocks and yarns.
The wealth and growth of this inland city are due
chiefly to the establishment and maintenance of the
immense flour mills, located on the banks of the
Mississippi River, which receive their motive power
from the Falls of St. Anthony, and their supply of
grain from the fertile fields of spring wheat in the
States of Minnesota, Wisconsin, and Dakota. There

are twenty-three of these mills, several of them built of granite, of a dozen or more stories in height, and of imposing architectural design; having a capacity, I am told, to manufacture thirty-seven thousand barrels of flour each day, and actually producing annually between six and seven millions of barrels, of which two millions are shipped away to provide the staff of life in foreign lands. Visitors are welcome at all times, and are treated with the utmost courtesy by proprietors and employés. I recognized my favorite brand, and followed the processes of its manufacture with extreme interest, from the emptying of the freight car contain-

HOME OF HON. W. B. WASHBURN, MINNEAPOLIS.

ing the freshly threshed wheat, through all the details of grinding, cleansing, and sifting, until it finally reached the muslin bag, and was sewed up and stamped.

Minneapolis is still in her "teens," but as beautiful as she is youthful, and, I am told, has determined to make her *début* this year as a rival to her elder sister, the enterprising St. Paul. While here we were the guest of our friend, Mr. T. L., who played the host *en vrai prince*, placing us in his phaeton, behind a pair of very rapid jet blacks, thus giving us an opportunity of seeing in a few hours what it would have taken us days to discover for ourselves. I was fairly amazed at the palatial residences; with the exception of perhaps half a dozen houses, New York has nothing comparable in the way of bold and tasteful architecture, combined with great solidity; the variety and combinations of colored stone particularly struck me, especially a remarkable blending of green and cream colors in one house yet unfinished, the unfortunate owner having come to grief during its construction. Its architecture was of the highest art, and I hope yet to see it in its completed magnificence. Perhaps the effect of these grand edifices, each built upon its own separate acre with its carpet of lawn and flower-beds, upon an eye accustomed to rows of brick and brown stone, is exaggerated as to the beauty of design and structure, nevertheless the Minneapolis homes impressed me with their splendor, and I cannot help feeling it is the most charming city I have ever visited.

Next day we made the tour of the chain of lakes which, with the surrounding land, constitute the people's pleasure-ground, or public park. Lakes Harriet and Calhoun are exquisite sheets of water bordered by wide and well-made boulevards and groves of trees; in fact, only just a sufficient contribution of art to preserve the beautiful gifts of nature, which is a great comfort in a world so given to strained efforts to compete with the Creator; yet where the handicraft and taste of man are essential, as in the construction of their massive public buildings, the people of Minneapolis are unsurpassed. The churches, libraries, banks, city buildings, office buildings, and newspaper offices have a most assured fire-proof and age-proof effect. The building of the Guarantee Company is wonderful: I was amazed when told that it had been commenced only a year ago, yet it has eleven stories, and is constructed upon the highest principles of architecture as to light, air and strength: there seemed to be nothing about it that had not its *raison d'être.* The view of the surrounding country from the top of it is simply superb, reaching to

"Where the Falls of Minnehaha
Flash and gleam among the oak trees,
Laugh and leap into the valley."

CHAPTER II.

AT five in the afternoon, May 16th, we once more find ourselves in a Pullman drawing-room, and as we have now to settle down for a three days' journey, it seems to us that the apartment has been made even more cosey than the one which brought us from New York; at all events, it has every thing that the most fastidious person could wish for, and when I compared it with the chilly, comfortless coaches in which I have been doomed to spend hours in Italy and Eastern Europe, I felt that those who grumble at the little *contretemps* that sometimes happen even in the wonderful Pullman system are a most unreasonable set; our compartment is a cute little salon by day, where we are happy in the *dolce far niente*, with our books, or in writing to those at home. We have every convenience, a cheerful and obliging porter, and when the white-jacketed waiter announces "supper is now ready in the dining-car," we simply walk through the vestibuled passage-way to the next car and are politely ushered to a tea which would have done credit to any home in the land. Just think of a broiled salmon steak, excellent and well-cooked chops, delicious waffles, strawberries, capital tea, and lots of other good things, if you preferred them, all for seventy-five cents; add to this, if you wish, a pint of Zinfandel (a California claret), and one dollar pays the bill. I really become so content and restful that I feel I could live here a month. Perhaps the men on the train miss their clubs in the evening, their billiards, or their rubber; but, as far as I am concerned, I am happy that there are no shops, no dinner parties, theatres, or balls. I live to confess that I do not miss them. Think of it, I retire at nine o'clock, and sleep peacefully until eight. I have but one *arrière pensée*, one nightmare: will I grow fat on this calm, heart-full, and stomach-full life? Yes, I have another: will the ubiquitous ten-months-old baby (there is always one to each car) yell in the night between the intervals of paregoric?

It is Saturday morning, May 17th, and I have slept deliciously; if the baby cried I was too unconscious to observe it, but about four in the morning I was awakened by a change in the temperature; it had become intensely cold, and I made good use of the extra blanket. Upon arising I find we are out on the treeless prairie, coated with a light fall of snow. For I should think two hundred miles we travel on in a straight line across this vast expanse of plain with no speck of foliage excepting here and there where the settler is making a fruitless effort to raise a few striplings; yet I am told that in a month these thousands of acres will be fresh and green with the young spring wheat, and what now is an uninteresting barren waste will then be a veritable cornucopia. What care I if the eye does tire of the monotony of the plain, the horizon, and the occasional farm-house? it can turn to the little dressing-room with its every convenience, its finely bevelled mirrors, tank of ice-water, marble basin with hot and cold water, and silver spigots, little shelves and trays in carved mahogany, adaptable to all the many necessities of a woman's toilet: a little *bijou*, which surely no *man* ever designed, unless he was a very, very much married man. Breakfast at nine—strawberries and cream, brook trout, broiled spring chicken, first-rate coffee. Think of it, and remember the old days, when we had to be elbowed and trod upon by rude men in the rush to get to the counter of the wayside station and choke or scald ourselves in the effort to bring on an attack of dyspepsia before the conductor should shout "All aboard!" Think of doing this on hot days, on cold days, on rainy days, and on slippery days, and then compare it with the decent, respectable, healthful method of to-day: a table for two, take your own time, rational meal, and the train carrying you on to your destination at thirty miles an hour: isn't it grand?

Breakfast finished, we find ourselves at Bismarck at 10 A.M., where the train stops long enough to permit us to take a stroll upon the platform and look at a busy

few
hese
, the
ding
opia.
y of
use ?
very
jes.
and
rved
of a
man
mar-
eam,
offee.
had
rush
hoke
tack
' All
cold
com-
thod
time,
your
nd ?
ek at
it us
busy

town built upon the trade incident to the great wheat country of which it is the centre. Here we lose the society of two sisters of charity, who have been passengers from Minneapolis, bound on an errand of mercy. I am sorry they leave us, for I feel better always for the influence of their presence; much as our faiths differ I have reason to have an immense regard, respect, and admiration for these dear good women, whose lives are full of sacrifice, immolation of self, and purity of heart. Bismarck is full of proud and tender memories for me. Seven years ago I leaned upon the arm of our great hero General Grant there

as we walked together to the ceremony of dedicating the State House, followed by a column of distinguished men, among whom were Mr. Villard, Mr. Evarts, members of the Diplomatic Corps, and others who were *en route* to the laying of the last rail to complete the great highway from St. Paul to the Pacific. Then, I rode over the Rocky Mountains 'n stages, ate terrible meals with all sorts and conditions of men, slept in the woods, got wet and dusty, frozen and broiled, according to the altitude to which we climbed, or from which we descended, and was more fatigued at the expiration of my four days' jolt than I would be in a Pullman car in a month. It was

on this occasion at Bismarck that I was witness to an
episode which is worth recording. Sitting Bull and
his chiefs, but recently stained with the blood of poor
Custer and his intrepid band of followers, were osten-
tatiously and indecorously paraded upon the platform
erected for the speakers, and Sitting Bull commenced
a harangue in his native tongue, which was being in-
terpreted, when the crowd below, now assembling and
realizing what was taking place, drove him with yells
and hisses to the rear and called Grant to the front. I
was in entire sympathy with the crowd. The picture
of the handsome Custer with his red scarf, as he dashed
along Pennsylvania Avenue on his runaway horse at
the grand review in Washington in 1865, was before
me, and so was his murderer. There was but one side
to such a ques-
tion. At all
events I can-
not work my-
self up to any
sympathy for
the Indian. I
have seen the
noble red man
at home, with
his filth and
his vice, his
dishonesty, his
cunning, and
his general un-

A BRIEF HALT.   (Kodak'd by Author.)

reliability, and I am among those who believe he should be coerced into good behavior and not tolerated as he is.

Leaving Bismarck we cross the muddy Missouri on a new iron bridge, and in twenty minutes are at Mandan, where a change of locomotives and conductors necessitates a halt of a quarter of an hour, giving us a chance to visit a curiosity shop of stuffed birds and beasts at stuffed prices, but as I have no use for these dust- and moth-catchers in my household, they tempt me not. Shortly we reach the "bad lands." I think the name belies them, for in addition to their being weird, picturesque, and puzzling, they are good grazing lands, as I myself can testify, if good fat herds of cattle afford any proof. The topography is of the most marvellous formation, and the colors are equally wonderful; here you see an ashy-gray hill of elephantine form, there a red cone as perfect as though just from the moulder's hands, again a pyramid, and then dozens of cones and pyramids, and this continues for a hundred, nay, two hundred miles. Often these quaint forms recall to mind scenes in other lands: once from the car-window I recognized on this arid desert the tomb of Cecilia Metella on the Appian Way, with its beehive formation and its battlements. Now and then you recognize what you believe to be an extinct volcano with lumps of scoria at its base, yet this may be only the slag or refuse of the burning lignite, which is frequently found and sometimes mined among these hills. What struck me as the most remarkable feature of this wonderful and enigmatic formation, was a series of well defined horizontal lines, a foot or two apart, which invariably marked the mounds or buttes, very much resembling the lines made upon the shore of a river by the rise and fall of the tide. Now I am not a geologist, nor gifted with much antediluvian or prehistoric lore, nor have I read any scientist's ideas of what I am describing, but to me it looks as if at some very remote period this entire region was the bottom of one or more fresh-water lakes as large as Lakes Michigan and Erie, or as small as those which cover acres of Wisconsin and Minnesota, and that by some process of evaporation, or by leakage or failure of supply, they gradually dried up, leaving these water-marks upon the hillsides to denote the periods of transition. At all events fossilized fish and shells are found here in abundance, and it is said that irrigation will make the soil productive. While I am thinking of it, however, and perhaps wasting my time in conjecture, we stop at Medora. Here is the wreck of a once thriving plant and settlement founded by Marquis de Mores, the husband of one of New York's rich belles, who conceived the idea that he could establish and successfully carry on at this place the business of raising and slaughtering cattle and sending the meat in refrigerator-cars to Eastern markets. He built a neat home, which can be plainly seen from the train, but after a serious altercation with some of the cowboys, resulting in a tragedy, in which the Marquis bore himself with considerable gallantry and nerve, he ultimately abandoned the scheme and left the country. Yet I am told by the people who should know best, that his plan was an excellent one, and will yet be carried out successfully, but lack of business experience and tact was the real cause of his failure. He established the fact, however, that cattle would fatten here, and that they could readily be prepared for safe shipment to the Atlantic seaboard, or "from ranch to table," as the Marquis epigrammatically styled it. He was a pioneer, and, like many others, perhaps a little ahead of his time.

HOME OF THE MARQUIS DE MORES.   *(Kodak'd by Author.)*

Looking at his house and the dismal surroundings, you cannot help congratulating the Marchioness that the scheme was a failure. No wealth would compensate for such a life to one accustomed to the whirl of the metropolis; *cela va de soi* it was a terrible sacrifice.

Another night of comfortable sleep and Sunday, May 18th, dawns upon us just as a spring day ought to—sunshiny, pleasantly warm, and a clear sky. This is to be a day of land- and water-scape, so we take our camp-stools and our Kodak to the rear platform and feast our better nature with a repast of the sublime and beautiful approach to the foot-hills of the Rocky Mountains. Here we have dashes of scenery to delight the most exacting artistic taste—mountain and ravine, valley and stream.; in fact, for the next twenty-four hours the track follows the meandering course of the great Yellowstone River, with its rapids and water-falls, its precipitous banks and rock-bound canyons,

its Indians and its cowboys,—an ever-changing whirl of panorama, through which we pass so rapidly that before the oft-repeated echo of our shrill whistle has

died away upon a scene of enchantment, another still
more beautiful surrounds us, effacing all recollection
of its predecessor, till the admiring eye and hungry
soul become satiated with a kaleidoscopic confusion of
the sublime. Asked now to select some gem for an
artist from among it all, I should fail; I could not par-
ticularize any special locality. If I had taken photographs one upon top of the other every five minutes of
that delightful day, and then made one composite picture of the whole, it might faintly convey an idea of
nature decked with her purple robes and
sceptre as it lingers in my memory while
I write.

At nine in the morning we reach Livingston, and here I experience the first and only
disappointment of my trip. This is the
entrance to the Yellowstone Park. Seven
years ago I left the train at this point and
went off on the little branch road to Cinna-
bar, and thence seven or eight miles in a
stage to the Mammoth Hot Springs. Oh,
ye geysers and yon lovely canyon, with
your marvellous waterfall, must I pass you
all by as I hurry on to Alaska? Alas, the
ship will be waiting for me at Tacoma, and
I have promised to be there.
Dear old Yellowstone Park, I
see plainly your snow-clad
mountains, I almost hear the
roar of your hot fountains;

"OLD FAITHFUL."

YELLOWSTONE FALLS.

"Old Faithful's" punctual coming and going is entitled to better treatment than I am giving him, yet I cannot tarry. Gladly would I walk there to feast upon those bright colors unseen and unheard of elsewhere. Oh, for one look from the summit into the deep abyss where soars the eagle, and for an hour beside those fathomless lakes of emerald mirrors and morning glories. But it must not be. I am exploring new fields. *Au revoir*, my old friend —so near and yet so far; if my life is spared I have not seen you for the last time; and yet we are such creatures of circumstances and conditions that I feel like exclaiming "*Lasciate ogni speranza voi che son entrate.*" Only a few years ago I rode with President Arthur, and General Sheridan, and Anson Stager, and Captain Clarke,

through the lanes and across the rivers of this wonder land. All gone! Yes, this hour is one of sad memories and disappointments; let me get back to the train and leave the past behind. From Livingston and through the Bozeman tunnel we arrive at Helena, the most thriving and populous city of Montana, located in the centre of one of the richest mining regions in the country. I spent some days there upon my previous visit, and spent them very uncomfortably; the accommodations were not fit for man or beast, much less for woman. All this, however, has changed since the completion of the railroad, and it now boasts of an admirable hotel (the Broadwater) and a luxurious and mammoth bathing-house. Leaving Helena we enter upon that wonderful system of railroad engineering which, I am told, is almost unequalled; here we commence the real ascent of the Rockies, circling around the sides of the snow-capped hills and leaping from crag to crag, over trestle bridges of dizzy heights and wonderful construction, culminating in the Mullen tunnel, which marks the summit, and emerging upon a beautiful valley just at sunset; abandoning the extra locomotive and rattling along at a lively pace on a down grade to Garrison, where there is a branch road to Deer Lodge, a beautiful little town with a nice, clean, well kept hotel, which gave me shelter and rest after my stage ride over the mountains in 1883, and thence to Butte and Anaconda, famous for their rich copper and silver mines. At this point (Garrison's), therefore, we lost many of our *compagnons de voyage*, who were destined for some of these places, and several of them to Salt Lake City.

To-day, in the dining-car, we were treated to a dinner which would have done credit to any first-class hotel in America, and which surpassed a great many dinners I have eaten in such so-called hostelries. I preserved the *menu* and here it is in full:

s for

com-

dmi-

mam-

upon

ich, I

e the

es of

crag,

erful

vhich

alley

d rat-

rison,

eauti-

otel,

ride

e and

silver

e lost

tined

Salt

a din-

class

many

s. I

DINNER, SUNDAY, MAY 18, 1890.

Potage à la Crécy,		Consommé Macaroni,
	Filet of Trout Princesse,	
	Potatoes, Dauphine,	
Cucumbers,	Radishes,	Olives,
	Boiled Ox Tongue,	
Grenadins of Veal,		Neapolitaine,
	Kromeskies of Lobster, à la Russe,	
	Peach Fritters, wine sauce,	
	Roast Beef, browned potatoes,	
	Roast Chicken, stuffed,	
	Curaçoa Punch,	
	Roast English Snipe,	
Boiled Potatoes,	Lima Beans,	Cauliflower,
Mashed Potatoes,	Stewed Tomatoes,	New Beets,
	Lettuce Salad,	
Fruit Pudding,		Sauce Labayon,
Rhubarb Pie,		Whortleberry Pie,
Vanilla Ice Cream,	Fruit,	Assorted Cakes,
Edam Cheese,	French Coffee,	Nuts.

If passengers are not served to their satisfaction, the fact should
be reported to the dining-car conductor.

All meals 75 cents.

I assure you it tasted just as good as it reads, and I enjoyed it thoroughly, epicure as I am.   The country we
are now passing through—that is, between Livingston
and Missoula, is a "dry section."   It seldom rains here,
and though the rivers and creeks run full, they are chiefly
dependent upon the melting snows in the mountains
for their supply of water. This gave us an opportunity
to see the method of irrigation adopted by the farmer to
water his crops ; it consists, as far as I could discover, in
damming up the streams and carrying the water from the
pools thus formed in little ditches to the grain fields ;
but the pools are only tapped at intervals whenever the
ground needs moisture, and I was told by an irreverent
passenger that this is a far more reliable system than
that provided by nature in the shape of rain.   Unfortunately the run west from Missoula was made at

night, and I was deprived of the satisfaction of once more enjoying a sight of the wonderful trestles which cross the ravines over which our train passes in its descent to the western side of the Rocky Mountains; one of them, the Marent trestle, which bridges the mountains across the Coriacn defile, being two hundred and twenty-six feet high; which is best realized by looking at the houses and occupants of the ranch immediately beneath it, who present very tiny specimens of architecture and humanity. I am glad that all these structures are now built of substantial iron; for on my previous visit the creaking of the timbers under the weight of our heavy train was any thing but pleasant.

MARENT TRESTLE, 226 FEET HIGH.

once
hich
r its
ains;
the
dred
ook-
nnie-
is of
hese
i my
the
sant,

NEAR CLARK'S FORK.

On the morning of May 19th, looking out of the
window at my bedside, I found myself emerging from
the rocky scenery of Clark's Fork, and afterward
traversing the edge of a beautiful sheet of water; so
hurrying with my toilet, I was soon out on the rear
platform absorbed in the charms of a panorama entirely unlike the wild rugged mountain scenery of the
day before. We were now on the banks of Lake Pend
d'Oreille. Whether it gets its name from the French
missionaries, who found the Indians indulging in the
harmless fashion of wearing earrings, or whether the
Indians named it themselves after acquiring a smatter-
ing of French, I know not, but I do know that, though
not "margined with fruits of gold," it was, when I
saw it, a clear lake, "glassing softest skies," and alto-
gether lovely; and it must be very large too, for we
were running alongside of it for fully two hours. It is
said to be the paradise of the sportsman, abounding in
bear, elk, deer, pheasants, wild fowl, and trout, and
I am told that in the months of September and
October the season is at its best. Some of this big
game, of course, I was not permitted to see, but I
can vouch for the trout, which I have eaten, and
for the thousands of wild ducks, which I have seen
there. The town of Hope, where we again set our
watches back one hour for the third time on our trip,
is said to be the head-quarters for the devotees of
gun and rod; it possesses a good hotel, experienced
guides, dogs, and all the other mannish things required
on such occasions.

the
rom
ard
: so
rear
en-
the
end
nch
the
the
ter-
ugh
n I
lto-
we
It is
g in
and
and
big
t I
md
cen
our
rip,
of
eal
red

The next point of interest reached is Spokane Falls, and it is indeed a point of very great interest. We have now left Montana and are in the young, thriving State of Washington, and this town — pardon me, I should have said city — will give the Easterner an idea of what can be accomplished by an industrious colony of American citizens where nature lends them a helping hand. Seven years ago, at the request of Messrs. Cannon and

SPOKANE FALLS.

Brown, two leading citizens of the place, I stopped over here a few hours (for we had a special train and loitered as we liked) to look at the magnificent water-fall. I do not think there were a dozen houses there at that time, yet to-day it boasts a population of over twenty thousand, all the result of utilizing the tremen-dous water-power of the "falls." I remember with

regret that upon that occasion these two gentlemen,
then in need of money, though now millionaires, offered
to sell their one-half interest in the water and the surrounding land to your father for $32,000, but he did not
avail himself of the opportunity; and yet five years
later a friend of mine gave more than this amount for
less than half an acre of this same land, and sold it at
an immense profit. Last year it was supposed to have
suffered from an extensive conflagration which swept
away the business part of the town, but to-day, as
magnificent edifices of solid masonry are replacing the
shanties of the past, the fire is conceded to have been
a blessing. I believe the day is near at hand when
Spokane will be a second Minneapolis, for it possesses
both the water-power and the crops which have made
the latter great. Up to this point, for three whole days
the eye has seen so much that is new and startling, that
it becomes weary just when the scenery grows flat and
uninteresting; in fact the millions of acres of sage-
grass and sand through which we now pass affords us
just the rest we need. I never fully realized until
now how true is the saying that we may have "too
much of a good thing," and if I took a nap from
Spokane Falls to Pasco, it was because I needed it
and was not missing any thing. When this desert is
irrigated and becomes a garden of orchards and flower-
beds, as is prognosticated by those who have the
hardihood and self-denial to live there, I am willing to
stay awake; but really I saw nothing worth describing
until passing through the promising towns of North

Yakima and Ellensburg we commenced the ascent of the Cascade Mountains. It is worthy of mention, however, that near Yakima is a very flourishing irrigated ranch, called the Moxie Farm, managed by Mr. Ker, which produces grapes and other fruit in great abundance and of the highest quality, and has proved so successful in the culture of tobacco that a manufactory has been established there, which is turning out what the men call "a high grade of cigar."

Monotonous as was this day's trip, there were many incidents which amusingly broke in upon it—for instance, at supper we found a stranger, who had come aboard at Pasco, looking indigenous to the soil, a good deal of which he carried upon his person; he was evidently dazed by the society in which he found himself, and did his best to adapt himself to the manners and customs of his fellow-passengers. Being handed a napkin, he carefully surveyed the company, and finding that some of the men had tucked their bits of napery in under their chins (a vulgar habit, by-the-by), he promptly did the same, and then, entirely unconscious of the object of so placing it, buttoned his coat over it, much to our delight and edification. Then he ate literally of every thing on the bill of fare, and when thoroughly gorged stretched himself out and picked his teeth with a resounding smack, the proud possessor of a lordly appetite and a digestion which would make countless thousands happy. And just here is a good place to say that sometimes coming late to our meals we find the colored porters seated at the tables taking theirs,

It seemed strange at first to me, but I must do them the justice to say that they behaved in the most decorous manner, neither eating with their knives, nor by any breach of etiquette or table manners doing the slightest thing to excite criticism: on the contrary, they could give lessons to many of the boisterous gentlemen (?) travellers who constantly jostled us.

Illustrating the straits to which the settlers are put upon their arrival out here, I cannot help speaking

of a queer little temporary structure which I saw built over a pile of fire-wood alongside of a tool-house on the railroad at Badger. It consisted of the show-bill of a circus and some pieces of old matting propped up upon half a dozen sticks, and perhaps would not have attracted my attention, but I thought I saw it move. True enough, just as the train moved on, a bright face emerged from beneath the show-bill, and, with a merry laugh, exclaimed "Ah, there!" Waving our adieus to the occupant of the improvised bed-tent, we wondered how long it would take him, in a country like this wonderful State of Washington, to pass through the stages which should bring him to the *otium cum dignitate* of a Queen Anne cottage and a porch.

Leaving Ellensburg we realize that we are coming to the end of our feast, and as night closes in on us we begin to look up shawl-straps and gripsacks, as we have to debark early on the morrow. Unfortunately the Cascade Mountains were crossed during the night, and we missed the wonderful feats of engineering which have made it possible for a train of cars to ascend and descend the Stampede Pass. I have seen it, however, on another occasion. It is simply marvellous, and with the exception of bits of the Denver and Rio Grande route there is no spot on the continent where the majestic work of the Creator is so skilfully supplemented by the ingenuity of man. For miles and miles you travel back and forth on the sides of these immense mountains to accomplish in the end a progress of only a mile or so in a straight line, looking down from the car window on the right at the track you have just passed over, and looking up from the window on the left to that which you have yet to surmount, while the wild torrent of a river rushes and plunges under you and over you and all around you, as though in angry indignation at your invasion, and a million stalwart firs, immense in height and thickness, stand as they have stood for centuries awaiting the doom which the little saw-mill in the valley is preparing for them.

At the summit we enter the famous Stampede tunnel, almost two miles in length, lit up by incandescent lights, in which we are imprisoned for eleven long,

very long minutes, and emerge to get a good view of
the switchback road, which for the two years preced-
ing the completion of the tunnel carried thousands of
passengers to and fro over its perilous timbers without
the loss of a single life. Here again we get a still
better view of the intricate and difficult feats of engineering than on the eastern side of the mountain, and

here we find the pic-
turesque Green River,
which stays by us un-
til we reach the level,
broad Puyallup Val-
ley, renowned for its
wonderful yield of
hops. Early in the fall
the hop-fields of this
prolific valley are a
charming sight ; the
lofty vines being laden
with the beautiful pale-
green flower, which is
plucked by Indians
who come long dis-
tances in their ca-
noes or on their
ponies in their pic-
turesque costumes

with their squaws, papooses and dogs, and camp like gypsies by the roadside, living on dried game and fish which they bring with them, and returning with enough coin to provide blankets and other necessaries for an entire year.

We arrived, on Tuesday morning, May 21st, at the city of Tacoma. And just here let me say that, much as I wanted to arrive at the port from which sailed the vessel that was to carry me to Alaska, it was with sincere regret that I left the comforts and luxuries of travel which I had experienced in that train from the Mississippi River to the Pacific Ocean.

THE WHARVES AT TACOMA.

CHAPTER III.

IN the summer of 1883 you will remember I was one of a party who visited Tacoma as the guest of Mr. Charles B. Wright, of Philadelphia, to whose sagacity I believe the Northern Pacific Railroad Company is indebted for the selection of this spot as the western terminus of this great highway. It was then a settlement (I cannot bring myself to dignify it with the name of town) of about 1,700 people. We reached it by rail along the grandly picturesque bank of the Columbia River from Pasco to Portland, and thence, partly by boat and partly by rail, to Puget Sound. Though I was not rude enough to confess it to my host, I do not now hesitate to say that it did not favorably impress me, and my three or four days' experience of its accommodations and food were anything but satisfactory. Its streets were unpaved and dusty, and as we drove through its principal thoroughfare our horses were compelled to meander around the

tree-stumps, still marking the recent existence of the
primeval forest. There were then but three buildings
of any pretensions in the place—a pretty Episcopalian
church, a young ladies' seminary, and a three-story
brick store. The only object of interest was the Old
Tacoma saw-mill, about two miles distant, and the
little town surrounding it, excepting when the clouds
lifted now and then to give a view of Mount Tacoma,
which process of lifting, by-the-by, never took place
while I was there at that time, so that I began to believe
its beautiful lines and its snowy hood were all a myth.

Seven years have come and gone, and seven times
five thousand people have come and stayed here since
then; not only stayed here, but they have prospered
and grown rich, and their wealth is now invested in
banks, manufactories, storehouses, handsome shops,
one charming hotel and many others of less pretensions, a university, two or three colleges, a dozen
school-houses and as many churches, a beautiful theatre, and every thing that goes to make up urban life.
Its society is simply delightful, composed of people
from the larger Eastern cities, many of them young
married folks, starting life and "growing up with the
country," but carrying with them to their far Western
homes such of the conventionalities and refinements of
city life as best secure the amenities which are indispensable to well regulated society, omitting only those
formalities which chill hospitality and dwarf courtesy
and good breeding into mechanism. "Come and dine
with us to-morrow at seven" sounds so much better
and heartier than "Mr. and Mrs. Status request the

pleasure," etc., etc., and yet when you sit down in one
of those charmingly furnished homes your reception
and your dinner are just the same as you have experienced in Beacon Street, Fifth Avenue, or Walnut
Street. The china, the glass, the flowers, the napery,
the cooking, and the wines would do credit to an
embassy at Washington, and the guests you are apt to
meet will generally have a store of knowledge quite as
gratifying to the reason as the viands are to the palate.

And what has brought about so wonderful a trans-
formation in seven short years? is the question which
naturally suggests itself as I marvel at the busy throngs
moving to and fro, and listen to the clatter of the
mason and the carpenter, and the whistle of locomotive
and steamboat. Let us see: standing upon the promenade of "The Tacoma" and looking out over Commence-
ment Bay, the first object to attract my eye is the
immense lumber mill of the St. Paul and Tacoma
Lumber Company, completely covering a piece of land
half a mile long at the mouth of the Puyallup River,
and giving employment in all its ramifications to five
or six hundred men. Beneath the bluff upon which
this promenade is built, I hear the rumbling and
shunting of the hundreds of freight cars laden with
stores from the East, which are here distributed over
the vast area of country known as "Puget Sound."
Far out in the deep water are a dozen or more large
ships waiting, I am told, for their turn to receive
cargoes of lumber or coal or wheat for England, Aus-
tralia, China, Japan, San Francisco, and South America;
some of them have brought cargoes of tea from the

Orient, others have just discharged iron rails and mer-
chandise after a four months' voyage around Cape
Horn. To the right I see the dense smoke and distinctly hear the noises which come from machine-shops
and foundries, and all around me I am sensible of a
restless activity pervading the people, whose lives
seem to be devoted to indefatigable toil. To a dweller
in the East who has been tortured by the slow process
of blasting and digging, of masonry and carpentry, of
plumbing and glazing and roofing, of papering and
frescoing, which postpone one's occupancy of his new
home until it becomes a question whether he will live
long enough to get into it, it is a sensation to watch
the evolution of a few loads of plank and boards into
a pretty Queen Anne cottage, as happens every week
in Tacoma; in fact, I know of one case (that of Mr.

VIEW OF PACIFIC AVENUE.

and Mrs. C. P., a newly married couple) where the
enterprising young housekeepers were residing in
their home in less than a fortnight after they had
selected a site for it. I cannot say they built it
from cellar to garret in ten days, for it had neither
one nor the other, but it had six rooms and a porch
and a shingle roof, and was not only habitable but
quite "stylish." "The Tacoma" hotel is well located,
and well kept, in all those respects which are independent of the vicissitudes and vagaries of labor. The
rooms are well furnished and so is the la.'er, but
whenever any thing went wrong, either with the
cuisine or the service, I found it attributable to the
difficulty of securing competent servants; in fact, this
trouble applies to all housekeeping, public or private,
in these new cities. The man who is intelligent enough
to make a first-rate waiter can do better in some other
capacity, and the women, I suppose, get married.
When I suggested trying the experiment of girls to
wait at table, as I have seen in my travels done very
successfully elsewhere, I was informed that they would
have to be both very old and very ugly, for there was
a great scarcity of brides.

Decoration Day came along while we were at
Tacoma, and I was agreeably surprised at the large
number of the veterans of the war who participated
in the parade, and the evident prosperity of all of
them. Near the head of the column rode my old
friend, General J. W. Sprague, who, General Sherman
tells me, was one of the very best commanders in his

army; and in the evening it was quite flattering to
hear my little book, "A Woman's War Record,"
spoken well of by the orator of the day. It is not
worth while pausing to think what would have been
the condition of this great Northwest country if these
brave men had failed, nor whether the Russian eagles
would not still be flying at Sitka; but I never look
upon their ranks and tattered flags without a patriotic
sentiment of gratitude for all they accomplished for us
and for posterity.

A few days may be well spent in Tacoma; there
are many interesting and pretty things to see, and the
distances are easily overcome by a system of electric
railways carrying you in every direction; and let me
say just here that the Western people from Chicago to
San Francisco are far ahead of us in their street railways. One would imagine that the object of these
conveyances is to carry you to your destination as fast
as is consistent with comfort and safety, and this does
seem to be the principle out West; but in the East,
for instance on the Madison Avenue Railway, which I
am compelled to use daily, the speed, if speed it can
be called, seems to be regulated to fatten the horses
and afford each passenger an opportunity to read a
novel or take a nap. The Annie Wright Seminary
for Young Ladies stands upon an eminence overlooking
the Sound, and has the reputation of being an excellent
institution. There is a similar school for young men,
and one or two colleges, perhaps universities, maintained by religious denominations. To those who have

a fancy for machinery and such things, a visit to the
Old Tacoma lumber mill and the one facing the hotel
will repay them. At the former I have seen huge logs
five, six, and seven feet thick, hauled up by immense
chains from the water, sliced into boards in a very few
minutes, and then rolled into ships through square
holes cut in their sides expressly for the purpose. A
street car runs to this mill from near the hotel, and
what I have described can be seen every day, and
ought not to be missed. By referring to my notes
I could tell you exactly how many millions of feet of
wood are cut here every year, but you would forget it,
as I have done; so I will run on and say that American Lake and Lake Steilacoom, which are both on the
same drive, and about twelve miles from the city, are
well worth a visit, not only because of their intrinsic
merit, but on account of the drive over the prairie
through the pine groves and along the level roads.
But the grandest sight of all, and certainly the most
fascinating north of San Francisco or south of Alaska,
is Mount Tacoma. I shall never forget the sensation
of its first dawning upon me—about the third day I was
in Tacoma. We were walking along G Street, near
the park, when my escort exclaimed, "Look at Mount
Tacoma," pointing in the direction to which I had
looked in vain from sunrise till dark in the hope that
the lowering clouds would dissolve or disperse and
open it up to view. Looking in the direction indicated,
my first impression was one of disappointment. To
my eye it was nothing but a very ordinary eminence,

still eclipsed by a very impolite white cloud which
completely masked its outlines. "Isn't it superb?" I
was asked. "Well, really, to be frank with you," I
replied, "I am terribly disappointed." "Then you
surely don't see it as I see it," was the response; and
as I began to follow the finger of my companion while

MOUNT TACOMA.

be traced out the mountain and separated it from the clouds which still hovered around it, I realized that the supposed white cloud was really the mountain itself; and as the atmosphere cleared and the rays of the setting sun covered its pure white slopes with a roseate glow, I became transfixed to the spot, gazing with all the wonderment of a child looking for the first time at some new creation he does not comprehend. "If I never see any thing else but that," I almost breathlessly exclaimed, "I am more than repaid for my two trips across the continent." Beautiful! grand! majestic! never-changing mountain! There you have stood, and there will you stand for all time, regardless of the mutations going on around you. Civilization may advance, barbarism may come again, sceptres may be shattered, governments may fall and new ones rise, calamity of war and flood may sweep pigmy humanity from the earth, but you will remain unchanged, immovable, to survive it all. It is not your curves, nor your crevasses, your glaciers, your tints, nor your deep unmelting snow, which fill me with awe and admiration. It is your eternal stability, typical of all that is steadfast in faith, in love, in hope. Oh, what a comfort to feel that you will still be here when I return from my visit to your sisters in Alaska, and that your face will be just as fresh, as glad, and as honest as it is today! Thanks, beautiful "Tacoma," for remaining out in the sunlight and the moonlight during the remainder of my stay within sight of you. How I envy the clouds, which have you so often exclusively to them-

selves! I heed not the whisper which tells me you
tower nearly 15,000 feet above the sea, any more than
I would listen to the cynic who analyzed the features
or the figure of an ideal woman. I can look at you
with the raptures of Shasta, and Washington, Mount
Blanc, and the Jungfrau still tingling in my nature,
but I yield to you the palm; I care not how tall or
how broad you are, or whether your deep shadows
and high lights are forests, or rocks, or glaciers; to me
you are peerless and unrivalled, like the Venus de
Milo, without prototype or antitype, absolutely unique.

PUYALLUP HOP-PICKERS.

CHAPTER IV.

THE steamship *Queen* was advertised to sail on the morning of Monday, June 2d, at four o'clock, so the passengers embarked on Sunday evening. We had already informed ourselves that she was a fine vessel, but were not prepared for the treat which presented itself as we drove down to the wharf to find a large ocean ship, splendidly illuminated from stem to stern with electric lights, awaiting us. Of course our curiosity was excited to visit all parts of the floating home that was to furnish us with all the comforts which exacting tourists demand, and naturally we first of all paid our respects to the saloon. Here we found every thing in apple-pie order—clean, neat, spacious, and thoroughly comfortable; in fact it was the counterpart of the saloon and social hall in the best of our transatlantic steamers. There were three tiers of state-rooms, all of them overlooking the water and none of them being what are known as inside rooms; a promenade extending over the whole length of the ship around the upper and lower tiers, and a seat or bench in front of every door, the whole being roofed in in such a manner that even in inclement weather you could live out-of-doors without the risk of getting wet. This being her first voyage for the season she was fresh, sweet, and clean, entirely free from the detestable ship odors that make some voyages sickening; and the china gloss of her new white paint as it mirrored the numberless incandescent lights, gave her a *fête-champêtre* effect which set us all to fraternizing at the very start and congratulating each other on the bright prospects ahead. I confess that I was not a little disappointed when I found that ours was one of the very tiniest rooms on the ship, contrasting so unfavorably with my spacious drawing-room in the Pullman car; but what was my surprise when I was politely told by the purser that as soon as the ship reached Port Townsend and took on the last batch of passengers, he would rearrange the rooms so that all should be perfectly satisfied, "for," he added "our instructions are to make everybody as comfortable as is possible." True enough, next afternoon we were changed to a very large and well located room, and given the use of the adjoining one for our baggage; and this incident serves to illustrate the uniform consideration and kindness which every one aboard experienced at the hands of both officers and servants, from the hour we left Tacoma until our return; and to those of us who are fond of travel and adventure this is a very important matter, for unless we find ourselves in a contented frame of mind, we are in no mood to appreciate the surroundings.

Of course you will want to know about the Captain. Well, I'm going to say what I think, regardless of the effect. The phrase may not be exactly what some women would care to set down in print, but it is expressive, and you will know exactly what I mean, when I tell you that Capt. James Carroll, of the *Queen*, is just as nice and lovely as he can be. It must be remembered that during the whole of the two weeks' voyage (with the exception of a couple of hours) we are within sight of land, more than half the time within a few hundred feet of it on each side of us, and as this is considered more difficult navigation than when out on the broad ocean, the Captain spent most of his time on "the bridge"; but when he did come to meals it was my good fortune to sit near him and to discover that he was still full of enthusiasm about the trip, though he had been making it for the best part of his life, and that nothing gratified him more than to feel that those around him were enjoying it, excepting perhaps the opportunity sometimes afforded him of giving them a good deal of useful information. I have often thought that a sailor may be none the less a sailor because he is courteous to his passengers; brusqueness is not essential to establish a reputation for discipline, any more than bad temper should go hand in hand with courage. I have known mild-mannered men who were the best of soldiers, and I have seen sailors who were as much at home in a drawing-room as in a gale. The story of the young man crossing the Banks of Newfoundland who innocently inquired : "Captain, is it always foggy here?" and got for an answer, "How do I know, I don't live here," may serve to lessen the number of absurd questions which would no doubt test the temper of the most amiable of seadogs, but it also serves to bring out in strong contrast those officers who have the tact, if not the natural inclination, to tolerate the curiosity of those of us who are really and sincerely in search of knowledge. When Captain Carroll did give us a specimen of that repartee which is a born trait of his countrymen, it was done to produce a laugh and not to humiliate. For instance, very thoughtfully, these ships are provided with a steam launch, which is carried on the lower deck ready for use if the vessel should become disabled, in which case the nearest assistance might be two or three hundred miles distant. The passengers, however, got the idea that this was a pleasure-boat to be used for little excursion parties in Alaskan waters, and one of the ladies, who was as much a favorite as she was a tease, and who delighted in having a little fun at the Captain's expense, asked him what he was going to do with the steam launch when we

Kodak'd by Author.

got to Alaska?" "Give her a coat of paint" was the quick response, and our fair friend enjoyed it as much as the rest of us.

Punctually at four o'clock, I am told, we left the wharf at Tacoma and headed up Puget Sound. Of course I was asleep, but upon reaching Seattle at six I was up and dressed, had taken a cup of hot coffee and eaten a biscuit brought to me by our room steward, who gloried in the *soubriquet* of "McGinty" (so called, doubtless, because he was very small and his hair was very red), and was ashore as soon as the plank was ready for us. Here we remained two or three hours, affording a too brief opportunity for a hurried visit through the streets of this phœnix city, which in a year has risen from the ashes of a fire which almost blotted it from the map. And what a city! Here was the same quick-step movement of the people which I observed in Tacoma as they hustled intelligently about, each one bent upon some errand of business—no idlers, no beggars—everybody doing something, and not enough to do it. Seven years before, as I remembered it, it was a town of some pretension as to size, but none whatever as to architecture. Now, the track of the great conflagration that in an hour had mowed down every business block in the place was recognizable only by the substitution of massive stone and brick buildings of the most modern type; the streets were newly and well paved; electric and cable railways were jingling their bells in all directions; the wharves and docks were dotted with

crowds of workmen and piles of goods; and a kind of
Mark Tapley temperament of being jolly under the
most adverse circumstances evidently pervaded the
community.

I should have liked to remain here at least a day
to have run out to Lake Washington, of which I
have heard so much; but all I could do in the little
time allotted me was to look with wonder upon

SEATTLE.

what has been accomplished since the fire, and to drop
into one or two of the shops, where a woman can generally get a fair idea of the inhabitants of a town by a
glance at the character and style of the things offered
for sale. If this is a reasonably reliable test, and I
think it is, I have formed a very favorable opinion of
the tastes and habits of the people of Seattle. All I

saw here was typical of American goaheadism. In
another year it will be known as a city of magnificent
buildings, and, like at Spokane Falls, the people will
realize that the recent calamity was after all a blessing.
The only thing that puzzles me is where the people are
to come from who will occupy the rooms of these lofty
structures. I see the supply, but ponder over the
question of demand, and am answered that it exists
already, and if it did not, the growth of this region is
so phenomenal that the supply of any thing and every
thing does not keep pace with the demand. It is certainly the paradise of builders, mechanics, and laborers
at present. Not the least interesting sight here was a
group of canoes, or "dugouts," occupied by Indians as
roving habitations. It was curious and instructive to
see the wonderful economy of space practised by these
people; a whole family, including cats and dogs, being
housed in a single boat. In one of them I saw two cats
and a dog, who had risen before the rest of the family,
eating their meal from a round tin vessel, which had
probably done similar service for the others at the
evening repast; while thus entertained I noticed a
movement giving evidence of life beneath one of the
blankets, and presently a member of the household
poked a pair of trousers under it, which so stimulated the
contortions going on within this open-air sleeping and
dressing room, that by-and-by a very sorry specimen of
the red man emerged, occupying the aforesaid panta-
loons, and demonstrating that the blanket had performed a very respectable and important function. The

rest of the family by degrees arose from their *boudoirs*
after going through similar movements, and when they
were entirely unmasked consisted of: a maiden very
much underdressed, in fact, not enough dressed for an
opera, who at once resumed her sewing where she had
probably left off the night before, the old man who
had acted as valet in distributing the wearing apparel
to the sleepers, an old crone in a scarlet and pea-green
dress, two little ugly children who had better never
been born, two cats, and a dog. There were a dozen of
these canoes, and this was a specimen of life upon each
of them. I don't know where they were going, as the
hop-picking does not take place until fall, but probably they had come down to trade their fish or their
furs for flour and groceries. At all events that is what
I was told, and if it is not exactly true it does not make
much matter. "*Si non è vero, è ben trovato.*"

A long blow of the whistle; an interval of fifteen
minutes and then another short blow; a shout from
the Captain instructing the men on the wharf to cast
off the ropes; a signal to the engine-room; a turn of
the engine, and we were sailing up the picturesque
waters of Puget Sound. The day was beautiful; it
could not have been better adapted to the use we were
making of it if it had been provided specially for us;
in fact during the whole fortnight that we lived on the
Queen we had the most charming weather—bright sunlight and cloudless skies—excepting the day of our
arrival in Glacier Bay, where it rained for a few hours.
In all this we were rarely fortunate, it seldom happen-

ing, I am told, that Alaska tourists are blessed with two whole weeks of what I call scenery weather. It is often foggy, frequently wet, and sometimes very cloudy; in addition to which the forests are periodically on fire, the atmosphere becoming so smoky that every object remains obscured until the fires are quenched by rain. Next to being born blind and doomed to listen to descriptions of what is going on around you, it must be the greatest torture to know that you are in the presence of the most beautiful works of the creation, hidden from you by a fog, and that you are speeding past them perhaps forever, never to return. I therefore hope the day is near at hand when it will not be necessary to remain on board the steamer and make the complete circuit of the coast whether it be fair or foul, but that you will be enabled to do it by easy stages, resting where you will at pleasant inns, and resuming your journey when the elements are favorable. Of course this kind of thing will come when the rush of sight-seers will not only warrant it, but make it necessary, yet I am well pleased that I have seen it all in its original and undisturbed grandeur, as I saw the Yellowstone Park before the introduction of hotels and stages.

Puget Sound is a grand sheet of water, several miles wide and I should think nearly two hundred in length; of course it is simply an arm of the Pacific Ocean, but so completely land-locked upon all sides excepting at its entrance, that it may be considered one vast lake affording absolute protection to the

ships which come here from all parts of the world.
It is full of beautiful islands, some of them rising
so precipitously from the sea that there is no foothold on them for man; others sloping down so gracefully to the water and dressed in such gorgeous colors
that you want immediately to buy one, and build a
house on it at the crest of the lawn. If you look at
them as links of a continuous chain, you perceive that
they are simply spurs of the Olympic Mountains
partially submerged by the ocean, and that if by some
convulsion of nature the water receded, the steamer
would find itself stranded at the base of a deep canyon
and surrounded on all sides by a range of mountains.
What most impresses you is the vast amount of timber
on all sides—trees of enormous height and thickness,
and such millions of them that you wonder how many
generations it will take to consume them. In my
school-days I knew nothing of Puget Sound excepting
that it was a speck of blue on the map somewhere up
by the North Pole; in fact no one else knew much about
it then (for that was *over* a quarter of a century ago),
yet to-day I am really afraid to write the names of the
many cities and towns which dot its shores, lest somebody should accuse me a year or two hence of having
overlooked many of them, for these cities grow up in a
spasmodic, startling kind of a fashion that takes your
breath away. Anacortes on Fidalgo Island has two
hotels, electric lights, a railway, and about three thousand people, all of which have come since last New
Year's Day. Fairhaven on Bellingham Bay is perhaps

twice as large as Anacortes, and is just one year old. Doubtless others are being born while I write, and may be ready for a place in my letter before I have it completed, if I don't make haste; and today I have a letter from your brother, now surveying a new line of railroad near Olympia, who says: "This place is growing so rapidly that I believe money invested prudently in real estate can be doubled in two months." The fact is, everybody has the fever to do something, and the wonderful development which this produces is attracting so much attention that capital and labor are both emigrating there from the East in such abundance that before the echo of the axe has died away in the forest, towns and railways, churches and schools, mills and factories, shops and homes, have taken the place of the stately firs, and a busy community is brought together to increase and multiply, and, I hope, to prosper. The number of steamboats one meets is also a great surprise; so are the crowds of passengers they carry. Among the former I noticed the *City of Kingston*, and the surroundings being not unlike the Hudson, I naturally thought of home, not with regret that I was not there again, but rather with pity for those who could and who did not come out to look at this wonderful and charming country.

BISHOP VLADIMIR.

At Port Townsend we stopped only long enough to afford Captain Carroll time to settle his business with the custom-house, this being the port of entry (whatever that may mean) for Puget Sound, and to take on the passengers who had come from San Francisco on the steamer *City of Topeka* to join us. And I am right glad they came, for their society was so enjoyable, and the narratives of their recent trips—some of them extending as far as the city of Mexico—so entertaining, that I am almost tempted to set their names down in print, even at the risk of being personal. I will simply mention, however, that among them were Bishop Vladimir, Archimandrite Innocent, and Rev. John A. Soboleff, of the Greek Church, who were on an Episcopal mission to Sitka.

(Kodak'd by Author.)

CHAPTER V.

AT five in the afternoon, after a very smooth run across the Straits of Fuca, with the horizon of the Pacific Ocean on our left, and innumerable picturesque islands on our right, we reached Victoria in British Columbia, situate at the extreme southern end of Vancouver's Island. When we were notified that we would remain here several hours, there was an immediate rush for the town, which was some three miles distant, our ship having stopped at the outer wharf in preference to entering the harbor; however, we found awaiting us several electric street cars, which rattled us off at a lively pace, and in a very few minutes set us down in the heart of the town. My previous visit to Victoria having impressed an indelible memory of a delicious dinner at the Driard House, I resolved to repeat the experience, and would have carried out my resolve, but was told that a visit to the "Poodle Dog" was quite the proper thing. Now the "Poodle Dog" is the name of a restaurant, but why, I am sure I cannot tell, and the proprietor was once, I believe, the *chef* of the Driard House. It is not an ostentatious looking place, yet it may be recognized by a very appetizing display in its windows of the good things in season with which it can supply you. On this occasion there were shrimps on show—beautiful, bright pink shrimps. As I was debating whether we would dine here or at the other place, the shrimps carried the day, so we entered the establishment, ordered dinner for eight o'clock, and then jumped into a victoria of another sort, and placed ourselves under the guidance of a not over-intelligent hackman. Fortunately (so thought the men), the shops were nearly all closed (in fact, I was told they open late and close early), so we started right off to do the town and its suburbs.

Oh, how smooth the roads were, and how nicely trimmed the hedges, and how neatly painted the garden gates—all *so* English, you know! and what an Eden of flowers! If you have never seen the English "May" in full blossom, you have a pleasure in store for you if you ever visit Victoria in *June.* How can I describe it! Its blossoms are either white or old-rose color, but the flowering is so luxuriant and compact, in fact so completely covers every twig of the tree, that they resemble a mass of white or pink carnations made into one huge bouquet as large as a cherry-tree. The air was full of floral perfume wherever we went, and the eye almost tired of the gardens of roses, laburnum, virginia, and the most gorgeous blood-red peonies I have ever seen. All this seemed to belong to Victoria as a matter of course. There was no effort at cultiva-

tion, no mechanical gardening; these flowers seemed to
thrive and to blossom because they couldn't help it.
To us in the East who have to take our plants in of
nights and put them in the nursery, even to sustain a
consumptive existence of a few brief days, it is quite
refreshing to plunge into the midst of a sea of flowers
as hardy and tenacious of life as they are delicate of
fragrance and of color. If I have ever looked at a
Claude Lorraine and doubted whether his pencil had
followed nature or his imagination the most, I shall do
so no more. Here was a theme of land-and water-
scape, incredible on canvas,—beautiful!oh, so beautiful!—beyond the reproduction of pen or brush,or even
camera.

Nature has been so prodigal of her bounty here
that it is difficult to turn even momentarily from
the green pastures and brilliant gardens to look at
some of the fine residences, yet we cannot help halting
for a moment at the one erected by the late Mr. Duns-
muir, with its castellated turrets and red roof surmount-
ing a magnificent structure of light granite, built on an
eminence which overlooks the city and producing a
grand architectural effect. Through the embryo park,
and past the barracks, we next drove up Beacon Hill
to the *point de vue*, and here our driver for the first
time stopped of his own volition; perhaps it was his
custom, perhaps he was himself a little dazed at
the picture which burst upon us all, perhaps his
horses were tired. At all events we find ourselves
upon a treeless lawn, furnished only with a flag-staff

and a rustic bench. The bench was partly occupied
by two gentlemen, who were so absorbed by the scene
before them that they hardly observed our coming,
or they would have made room for us; so we remain in our carriage and gaze in quiet, speechless
wonder at the exquisite picture before us. The land
slopes away at our feet, making green sward, then
come a few of those exquisitely colored gardens of
which I have spoken, then a piece of woods, and
finally the rock-bound coast with its splashing and mur-
muring waters; beyond this the placid lake-like land-
locked sea, studded with innumerable islands and
dotted with boats and sails and steamers meandering
and tacking their way here and there through the
intricate channels; beyond these the deep blue foot-
hills of the Olympic range fringed at their base by the
royal and stately fir, and beyond all, towering through
the clouds skyward, the snow-topped giants of the
North Pacific coast. It was now nearing eight o'clock,
which in this latitude and at this season is the time
that the sun disappears, though for two hours more he
illuminates the atmosphere with a pleasant twilight
and tinges all nature with "rare and roseate shadows."
We saw these tints and quickly changing colors in all
their phantasmal mystery: now prussian blue fading
into ultramarine, then being lit up by a ray of yellow
from the horizon suddenly changing to a pale green,
while the snowy summit lines of the Olympic range
were tipped with opal, and finally, as the outline of
the mountains grew faint, a single streak of liquid fire

marking the line where the ocean seemed to melt away.
It was a veritable scene of enchantment, and we left it
with such reluctance that our eyes and our souls faced
backwards and lingered with it until our carriage had
turned abruptly towards town and it was lost to view.

On our way back your
father could not resist
the desire to alight and
ask the names of the
many plants and blos-
soms which decorated
the pretty homes we
passed; and this he did
of a party of young peo-
ple indulging in lawn
tennis, who not only
gave him the informa-
tion with bright intel-
ligence and welcome

phrases, but insisted upon loading him with both arms
so full of exquisite flowers that when he returned to
us we hardly could find room for them in our carriage.
I shall not soon forget the gentle and suave courtesy
with which our simple request for information was
responded to by the gentlewomen and youths, whose
merry-making we broke in upon, and I was glad afterward to learn the name of the head of the household,
whose surroundings and refinements were in accord
with such good breeding.   If this page ever comes to
the eyes of any members of Mr. R. C.'s family, and

they should happen to remember the Yankee invasion I refer to, I hope they will believe that my little group was thoroughly impressed by their kindness in this episode.

> " All human history attests
> That happiness of man (the hungry sinner),
> Since Eve ate apples, much depends on dinner!"

You are right, Lord Byron! but when you wrote "the mountains look on Marathon, and Marathon looks on the sea," I doubt very much while "musing there awhile," you would have tolerated an invitation to a dinner even at the "Poodle Dog"; yet let me assure you that if you had sent a regret you would have made the mistake of your life.

The "Poodle Dog" is presided over by M. Marbœuf, who is a cook of excellent merit, as I can testify, being quite a *cordon-bleu* myself. We were shown to a little apartment in rear of the store, which seemed devoted principally to the ice-cream eaters, and found a table with covers for three, prettily decorated with radishes, olives, and shrimps, and a few bright roses. I need not confess to you my daughter that much as I delight in exquisite scenery and admire works of art, I take a great deal of pleasure in gratifying my taste for good living: a drive in the Bois is none the less enjoyable because you know that a lunch is ready for you at the Cascades; the deep blue of Murillo in the gallery of the Louvre is perhaps appreciated with more enthusiasm if you expect by and by to season your fatigue with a dinner at the Café Anglais, or Vibert's, or the

Riche; and the labor of the ascent of some Alpine
pass is compensated for not exclusively by the gorgeous surroundings of the hour, for without the cold
chicken and flask of native wine, wrapped so neatly in
the white napkin and packed snugly away in a cute
lunch-basket, there would be an element of self-sacri-
fice about it that would make you feel you had
performed some deed of martyrdom. I have, therefore, made it a rule of my travels that my palate
and my gastronomy should be well cared for, if possible, in order that I may keep on such good terms
with myself as to receive the various impressions
of my journey in an amiable and contented mood.
So much for the philosophy of my dinner at the
"Poodle Dog," and now for the realistic part of it.
The *maître d'hôtel* served it *in propriâ personâ*,
and the meal was opened with the shrimps as an
incentive to appetite, I presume; if so, they well performed their mission, for we were all seized with an
appetite for—more shrimps; following these came
Olympia oysters, in the shell, not one of which was
larger than a nickel, with only just a delicate suggestion of the coppery flavor which, to my uncultivated
taste, spoils the English "native"; and now, while we
were busy with a broiled spring chicken,—and such a
chicken, so white and so tender,—our good host informed us that he had forgotten when we inquired for
game that he had a squab pheasant in the refrigerator,
and he would cook it at once, if we desired. "Roast
it before the fire, and serve with bread sauce," was the

prompt response of one of us; "and bring a bottle of this Château Margaux 1864," said another, handing the wine list to the waiter; and while the pheasant is being trussed and roasted we linger over our chicken and delicious California asparagus and *soufflé* potatoes. It was perhaps half an hour before our *pièce de résistance* was ready, but it was well worth waiting for; it seemed to me that the untimely demise of that youthful bird was fully atoned for by the manner of his presentation in the form of food, as he appeared impaled through the breast by a silver skewer, surmounted by the lion and the unicorn entwined with a cordon of alternate mushrooms and truffles; and with him came a lettuce salad with a *soupçon* of onion and *estragon*, fit "to set before a king"; the strawberries which followed had just been picked from M. Marbœuf's garden, the cherries I have never seen excelled, excepting in Germany, and the coffee was made by a Frenchman, which is all that is necessary to say about it. This ended the feast, save the ceremony of settling for it, and I deem it my duty to those who follow me hereafter to say that though the dinner was as well served and cooked as it could have been at Delmonico's, and in some respects perhaps a little better, yet the prices were not only exorbitant but extortionate. I would therefore advise that a full understanding be had with the proprietor in advance, lest you find yourself charged four dollars for a bottle of claret marked three on the list, and about five cents apiece for shrimps, of which you will probably eat two dozen

if you are fond of them. However, we did not permit
the bill to disturb our equanimity. The moon being
at her full, and several of our shipmates being in the
same condition (I refer to the eatables only), we
resolved to get back to the steamer on foot, and thus
perhaps avoid the nightmarial attack which we had
been inviting. It was a jolly tramp, along a level
board walk of three good miles. The young men sang,
as did some of the old ones too, while the women
laughed as they listened to the misfortunes, set to
music, of an Irish gentleman who had a mania for
tumbling into horrid places, "dressed in his best suit
of clothes." When we reached our bright, beautiful
ship, she lay like a luminous palace beckoning us on to
sweet dreams and the *dolce far niente* of her life.

CHAPTER VI.

DAYLIGHT was tinting the landscape when we resumed our voyage, and, as I had resolved at the start that I would only sleep when I could not see, I was up and walking the deck before six o'clock, filled with a sense of pity and regret, to use no harsher term, for those who still remained in bed. Your cup of coffee and biscuit are always ready for you at the tap of your electric bell, so that no excuse about "not liking to get up early because you have to wait so long for breakfast" avails you one particle. If you do not prefer what I am looking and wondering at to the comfort of sleep (which is an excellent thing in its way), by all means remain in bed, so that the few who are enjoying the effect of the sunrise may have plenty of elbow-room. Let us see who are those who are around our little group of three, sharing with us the pleasant breeze and balmy sun-rays of this exquisite June morning. I see Miss Margaret W., from Illinois, and Miss Marian B., from New Jersey, each with their

Kodaks, waiting for a chance to snap something—bright,
good girls both of them, and I wish them both good
snaps. There, too, the ever-smiling features of Mrs.
H., from San Francisco, her graceful form hurriedly
thrown into an ulster, and a little scarf carelessly encircling her throat.   On the upper deck is the Rev. C.
C. Tiffany, of New York, and his cousin, Miss J., with
their field-glasses,
probably talking of
Japan, the Yosemite
and the Norwegian

midnight sun; near them, Mr. Drake and Mr. Sherman,
from St. Louis—great travellers, and both fond of it;
Mr. and Mrs Meinertzhagen, from London, who have
spent the first two years of their married life travelling
around the globe, and tell us they have yet one more
year to devote to it, who are now doing Alaska
for the second time; Mr. Duhring, of Philadelphia; Bis'op Vladimir and his associates, speaking

Russian; Miss D., also a great tourist and always wide-awake when any thing of interest is to be seen; Mr. John Bernhardt, a German gentleman in charge of a gold mine in Alaska, who wishes he wasn't; and three or four others whose names I do not know. The young men who were playing whist until midnight of course would be in no condition to resume the game after lunch if they lost their rest, so they are not with us, nor are those who take two hours at their toilets; but those of us who travel with our eyes and ears wide open are here, and we have no regrets. This is the Gulf of Georgia, the land on the left is the Island of Vancouver, that on the east is British Columbia, and both shores remain distinctly visible for two hundred and fifty miles of our journey, though the Gulf of Georgia narrows into Johnstone Straits after we have sailed half that distance. It may be interesting to mention, though it is no part of my intention to write either history, geography, or ethnology, that Vancouver gets its name from an officer of the ship of the great navigator Captain Cook, who took peaceable possession of the island in the name of the English government just one hundred years ago, and rendered inestimable service to mariners in surveying and publishing charts of the coast; also that the ownership of the island of San Juan, on our right, was the subject of dispute between England and ourselves as late as 1872, when, during General Grant's presidency, the question was referred to the German Kaiser as arbitrator, and decided in our favor.

We are sailing on a perfectly smooth sea, without a ripple save the foamy furrow of our ploughing through it at the rate of fifteen miles an hour, and the long line of agitation with which our propeller marks our wake. Standing at the bow for a quarter of an hour we penetrate, either with the naked eye or our glasses, a vista of superb tranquillity; passing to the starboard side we find ourselves over-looking a placid bay encircled by forested mountains of prodigious size and snow-capped in the distance; crossing through the social hall to the port side we are in the midst of an archipelago of a thousand islands of emerald green and crimson, looming up in the most fantastic forms, some round, some oblong, all clothed with a rich carpeting

of verdure, or wrapped in the thick foliage and warmth of the ever-present fir; and then to get one fond last look as we hurry along so fast, so horribly fast, we walk briskly to the stern, where, overlooking the frothy water, lashed into foam by our wheel, we find that these beautiful mountains, islands, and forests have closed in upon us like one vast frame, leaving no trace of the course we have taken since we left Victoria.

It is a shame to be disturbed at such a moment and in the midst of such an ever-changing panorama by the sound of the breakfast bell, but the

(Kodak'd by Author.)

meals on the good ship *Queen* are always so excellent, so hot, and of such variety that I must go down. I sometimes wished they were quite bad, that I might feel it no hardship to skip a few of them, but, like every thing else on this glorious trip, they are above criticism. Moreover, this morning I had the pleasure of meeting, at breakfast, Mrs. G., the wife of the Mayor of Victoria, who had joined us for the cruise at that city. We had been

informed that our first stopping-place after leaving
Victoria, would be Nanaimo, but at breakfast we were
told by the captain that that would be reserved for our
return, as he would have to stop there twelve hours for
coal, so we pushed on through these wonderful islands,
twisting and turning as the necessities of navigation
required, I suppose, each change of our course opening
up some new scene of enchantment and the next one
closing it to view, leaving nothing behind but the hope
that another turn would bring it back, and then quite
suddenly experiencing a realization of our wish. Making myself comfortable on the very uppermost deck,

clad in an ordinary cloth
walking-dress, with a little
astrakhan jacket over my
shoulders, I just sat and
revelled in this monotony
of constant change, and let
my fancy wander through a
score of delicious flights of
imagery. Looming up be-
hind these immense woods,
which, I am told, are themselves growing on hill-sides
one thousand feet above the
water, I see miles and miles
of mountain and table-land
covered with snow, the
depth of which can be appreciated with the naked eye;

(Kodak'd by Author.)

there they stand like the palace abodes of some giant
race with their façades of purest marble, their turrets,
their windows, and their towers; my imagination
takes me to Greece, and I stand below the steps of the
Acropolis; I am once more in Rome, entranced by the
silent magnificence of the Coliseum, and as we pass
around the point of another island and I get a glimpse
of what looks to me like an avalanche of snow curving
over a shelving rock into the abyss below, I think of
home and our own Niagara. I am told that exciting
scenes produce different effects upon our natures
according to the character of what is transpiring;
for instance, that soldiers never speak to each other
during battle, the only voice heard being that of
command; I myself in a panic at sea have seen a
whole crowd paralyzed into speechlessness; at a
railroad accident or a fire where loss of life is threatened, they say men run aimlessly about shouting to
each other, but none of them doing much that is useful; and I observed on my Alaska excursion a nervous
impulse produced by the excitement of the voyage
which took the form of running around the ship and
calling your fellow-passenger's attention to something
that could only be seen at some particular spot.
"There's a whale," says somebody, as a spout of
water is suddenly thrown ten feet in the air and is
repeated at regular intervals; and instantly the little
crowd disperses itself wildly all over the ship shouting
"Come and see the whale," which in five or ten minutes
becomes "*Have* you seen the whale?" and then in half

an hour, "*Did* you see the whale?" And thus you are
kept informed of water-falls, seals, porpoises, salmon,
eagles, and Indian canoes, till the day slips by with
nothing specially to mark it, but with the mind satu-
rated with the wonders of nature just as it is with those
of art after a day spent at Versailles or the Vatican.
And yet as I retire I am told by Mr. B., the German
gentleman, who has left at home a jewel of a wife and
a cluster of little ones whose pictures he has shown me,
and has spent a winter in Alaska (it makes me shiver
to hear of it), that to-morrow will be a much more
interesting day.

June 4th.—Can it be possible that it has been only
two days since I left Tacoma? and I have done Seattle,
Port Townsend, Puget Sound, Victoria, the Gulf of
Georgia, and all those beautiful things which, for your
sake, I wish with all my heart I could describe, but
which you must see for yourself to realize how poorly
the very choicest language would paint them. This is
another lovely day, which I confess is a complete
surprise and a most agreeable one, for we had been
cautioned against making the trip so early, as we would
undoubtedly strike what the sailors call "dirty weather."
But no, there is not a speck of cloud, not a puff of
wind, just the same balmy atmosphere as that of yesterday, and nothing to indicate that there ever is any
weather in this region save the streaks of cobwebby
mist that here and there lace themselves in among the
trees or around the rocks for a few minutes and then
dissolving into moisture under the warm sun, disappear:

and we would not be without these for the world, for
they are exquisitely picturesque, as delicate and ephem-
eral as the smoke of a cigar,
and so shy that at the blowing
of the whistle they seem to
weep themselves to death. We
have passed through Johnstone
Straits in the darkness, which
I much regret, for I am told
the channel is very narrow and
the sides very high and precipitous, but it is some comfort to
learn that there is little or no
difference between that and the
scenery we are now passing
through; yet, why cannot it
be so arranged that the ship
should anchor at bedtime and

start again at sunrise? It is too bad that the least
bit of it should be missed, and we only hope that the
captain will so time our movements that we may see
it coming back. The feature of to-day's experience
is the wonderful transparency of the water; as we
peer over the bow of the ship it seems as though we
could see down into the ocean fathoms deep; in fact it
is not like water at all, there is nothing I can compare
it to but the clearest plate glass of immense thickness
and unsullied purity.

IMAGE EVALUATION
TEST TARGET (MT-3)

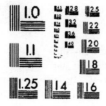

CHAPTER VII.

THE fourth day out from Tacoma (June 5th) we found ourselves, when we came from our state-rooms lying at the wharf at Fort Wrangell, the United States war vessel, *Pinta*, being very near us, and the small boats of both ships plying to and fro exchanging civilities. This place gets its name from Baron Wrangell, who was the Russian governor of Alaska when the few fishermen who had settled here grew numerous enough, about the year 1834, to dignify their local habitation with a name; subsequently it grew up into a place of considerable consequence and population by reason of the discovery of gold in the vicinity, but when these mines ceased to be profitable, fell into a condition of

FORT WRANGELL.
(Kodak'd by Miss Margaret Watson.)

decay which seems to possess it still. More recently it has been a United States military post, but even the glamour of the few bayonets has departed, and Fort Wrangell is perhaps to-day as uninviting a spot as any in the world, save for the few curiosities in the way of Indian graves and totem poles,

TOTEM POLES AT FORT WRANGELL.

and the very excellent work being done by the missionaries in the Indian schools. As I landed, I met and was presented to the Governor of Alaska (General Knapp), who was making a tour of the coast on the *Pinta*, and who was dressed in the uniform of a major-

general, minus the shoulderstraps. The morning was
cloudy and chilly, with occasional showers, very much
in keeping with the few dreary streets and abandoned
huts which go to make up this old western fortress of
the Czar. The fort itself or stockade was an utter
wreck; in fact I would not have known of its ex-

A STREET IN FORT WRANGELL.

istence if left to discover it for myself, so I hurried on,
picking my way as best I could through the muddy
thoroughfares to get a view of my first totem pole. I
assure you my initial experience of a promenade in an
Alaskan city was far from agreeable, and several times
I wished myself back in our good ship, where I could
view the rocks and the trees from afar off, rather than

be bruising my poor feet upon the one, and crawling over the prostrate forms of the other. It was evident that the place was entirely without horses and vehicles of any kind, for the principal street—if street it may be called—was grown a foot high with grass, and was chiefly used as a place to store canoes and firewood; there evidently had existed at some distant period a plank sidewalk, which ran along the entire front of the village, but time had played such havoc with it that the people now walked in the street to avoid it. It seemed to me as though there was not energy enough in the whole place to light a fire on a cold day.

But I saw the totem poles; and since that time at various other places have seen them, and pictures of them by the score, and although I confess there is little about these totem poles which is at all attractive from a physical point of view, they are interesting in so far as they illustrate the fact that all humanity, even in its aboriginal and its

barbarous state, adopts for its own protection certain
rules and laws of government. The totem pole of the
Alaskan Indian is his crest, his family name. He is
a "bear," or an "eagle," or a "salmon," or a "crow," or
a "whale," and being so he owes certain duties to his
kin, the chief of which is that he may not marry a
member of it; and another, that any crime he commits
attaches a responsibility to his entire class, even as an
injury to him is an injury to his whole stock. In the
one case all may expect to suffer, in the other all must
be ready to avenge. And this totem-pole custom leads
to extravagant display of family pride among those
who are well off. It is as much an evidence of prosperity for Mr. Bear to erect a high pole surmounted by
a poor imitation of his god-father and carved on all
sides with rude effigies of his ancestors, as it is with us
to live in a palace; and I wondered as I looked at some
of these horrid sculpturings whether they did not be-
get the same neighborly jealousy and vulgar rivalry
which possess those who esteem themselves more civilized. The people must devote a great deal of their
time to carvings of this character; it seems a mania to
be shaping a piece of soft pine into their family name,
just as it is with other people to scribble theirs all over
the world, from the pyramids of Egypt to Indepen-
dence Hall. For the information of our Darwinian
friends, I may as well say that I was unable to detect
the monkey among any of the ancestral specimens.
Since the Indian has come into contact with the pale-
face he has adopted those of our traits and customs

which he approves, among them being exchanging any thing he has for money; and another, drinking as much whiskey as he can get; and although there is no case on record, perhaps, of one of these people selling his family tree, yet he makes miniature representations of it all winter and sells them to the tourists in the summer. One of these I have, which was purchased under peculiar circumstances at Juneau and will be told of hereafter, and I procured at Wrangell a very grotesquely carved effigy of an Indian Shaman (medicine man or doctor), of whose calling I may have occasion to speak by and by. I visited some of the huts in which these families, whose creed so carefully guards their ties of consanguinity, reside, and there can be nothing worse in the slums of London than what I saw here. In the centre of each was a space of about a yard wide in the floor, upon which were the fires for warmth and for cooking, the only escape for the smoke being through the roof, where an aperture was left for that purpose. Two or three families were squatted in a circle around this fire, the men appearing to be clothed in the cast-off wearing apparel of the white man, and the women tightly wrapped in skirt and blanket, lying full length

(*Kodak'd by Miss M. D. Beach.*)

upon the floor, the shoulders slightly elevated, their
coppery faces and straight long hair protruding from
the blanket and lit up by the whites of two staring
eyes, for all the world like seals in a menagerie—
but with a heart-rending expression of misery. The
Siwash woman is a beast of burden. If captured in
war, she becomes a slave and a drudge to her captors
for the rest of her life; if living with her own tribe,
she is none the less a serf to the man whom she calls
her husband, and who leads a life of indolence and vice.
It is therefore a common habit of these poor wretches
to murder their female offspring at their birth, and
thus save them the inheritance of a life of toil, shame,
and misery. But if a girl escapes being the victim of
infanticide, a much worse fate awaits her on her arrival
at womanhood; she is often then sold for a few blankets
to the highest bidder, and here commences a life which
would seem to justify, if any thing could, the murder-
ous act of the mother. Polygamy is practised among
all the tribes, and in some localities a man increases his
wives just as he would purchase oxen or horses, to till
the fields; the greater the number of his wives, the
greater amount of work he can accomplish. The odors
in these huts were stifling, and the filth so alarmingly
dangerous that I had little opportunity to investigate
the board or the lodging; but in one of them I saw an
old man dying, a woman lying ill with a fever, a whole
brood of children some of whom were crying, and a
couple of shaggy dogs; all this life and sickness and
death being the state of existence of a single family—

a horrible picture of squalid misery and misfortune, which made me feel like asking with Dante : "*E' che gent'è, che par nel duol si vinta?*" But the missionaries are at work—in fact, they are doing splendid service here and elsewhere, and although I did not visit the school at Wrangell, owing to the indisposition of one of our party, I had a grand opportunity to see one next day at Sitka, and shall give you a full account of my experience when I come to it. There are some remarkable typical Indian graves in the vicinity of Wrangell, which are well worth visiting; had the weather been brighter I should have made an effort to see them, and I certainly should have gone anyhow if there had been any mode of conveyance, but there was absolutely none. The totem pole, however, is the chief feature of them, serving the purpose of headstone and inscription. Longfellow, you will remember, has it thus :

" And they painted on the
   grave posts
Of the graves yet unforgotten,
Each his own ancestral
   totem,
Each the symbol of his
   household—
Figure of the bear and reindeer,
Of the turtle, crane, and
   beaver."

Perhaps the most curious thing
to be seen in the village is the

hull of an old steamboat, high and dry in the main
street, whose decks are boarded and roofed in
and divided off into apartments for use as a hotel,
and although there was little vestige of human life
about it upon my visit, I was told that during the
mining boom up the Stickeen River it had been a very
popular hostelry. I was glad to get back to the *Queen,*
her clean decks and the ablutions which the comforts of my stateroom afforded, and gladder still to see
the clouds break away and give presage of a bright
afternoon and morrow.

It is the custom of the ships, after leaving Fort
Wrangell, to proceed next to Juneau, then to Chilcat,
Glacier Bay, and Sitka, but we did not follow this
course. Captain Carroll, finding that the night was
going to be clear and the sea smooth, took a westerly
course through Sumner Strait (formerly called Duke
of Clarence Strait), around the south of Baranoff
Island, and thence north to Sitka, keeping the island
on our right and the broad Pacific Ocean on our left.
Having announced this programme to his passengers,
we went to lunch to chat it over, where the captain
was voted a most accommodating host; and we naturally fell into a conversation touching our first visit to
an Alaskan town, during which I became indebted
both to Captain Carroll and many of the intelligent
people I met at his table for a good deal of valuable
information touching the manners, habits, and customs
of these Indians, much of which was subsequently
verified at Sitka. As you depart from Wrangell you

get a superb view of the mouth or delta of the Stickeen River. It was far up this stream that the Cassiar gold mines were discovered, which promised so much for the prosperity of Wrangell, and great faith still exists among the people as to the future mineral wealth of the far back country.

The sun was now beginning to make himself felt in real earnest, and the atmosphere changed to that mild, balmy sort which all who have written about Alaska seem to agree exists in this vicinity, but which I had despaired of experiencing. The clouds had dried their tears and departed, but the beautiful fleecy vapor in straight, trans-parent, cob-webby lines still hovered amidst the tree-tops, just as a bit of fog will cling to the masts of a ship for many miles; in some places it looked so like the linger-ing steam from a quick-moving locomotive that I began to ask myself how soon the shrill whistle and the rushing racket of the steam engine would resound along the banks of yon-der river, freighted with the precious nuggets

THE STICKEEN DELTA.

now lying hidden in the mountains, which, unfortunately, I have not the clairvoyant power to find.
The Stickeen Delta is a beautiful picture, of which I
was unable to get a Kodak copy, as the atmosphere
did not clear until we were too far removed from it,
and the one I give you on page 85, which I obtained
elsewhere, does meagre justice to it. This afternoon
was spent chiefly in walking the upper deck; the
thermometer was 70 degrees in the shade, and the
Kodak fiends were at work everywhere
preserving as best they could the counterfeit presentments of each other—my party
among the rest; and although it was our
first experience, and we had little faith in
our ability to ac-
complish much, we
have been most
agreeably disap-
pointed by the re-
sult, many of our
photographs of the
scenery and groups
being perfect gems
in their way. Din-
ner came and went,
and we were again on
deck. The scenery continued

(Kodak'd by Author.)

to be superb—in fact, it grew even more sublime the
farther north we went, the snow-hoods of the mountains became thicker and hung lower, the blue of the

foot-hills became more intensely blue, and the crimson
and yellow of the ferns and grasses grew luxuriantly
picturesque. It was still daylight, but the outlines were
growing fainter and the air chilly, so that some of us
were arranging to spend the remainder of the evening
in the saloon, when, to our surprise, we discovered that
it was already ten o'clock—bedtime, in fact—but the
novelty of daylight at such an hour was so agreeable
that few of us retired. We did a much more sensible
thing in procuring an additional wrap and standing on
the bridge until midnight, interesting ourselves with
the beautiful steering of the ship through the thousand
islands which are sprinkled all over the ocean in front
of Sitka, where we arrived just at twelve o'clock, and
dropped the anchor a little distance from the city.
The Sitkans, it appears, had seen us for several hours,
but of course did not recognize our ship, as this was
her first trip to Alaska, and, moreover, we should not
have been due there for several days if we had followed
the beaten track of the excursion boats. We were the
first lot of tourists to arrive that season, and when at
last the truth was heralded from house to house, there
was intense excitement: first, among the American
residents, to whom the faces of their countrymen are
as welcome as the life-boat to the shipwrecked sailor;
and second, to the Indians, who realized that "to-
morrow will be market-day." We were soon surrounded
by all sorts of canoes, dug-outs, row-boats, and sail-
boats; and midnight though it was, the natives had
brought with them their wares, and the white people

were willing to sit up the rest of the night if they could only get a newspaper even a month old. There was among this remarkable fleet a little steamer which afforded us a world of fun ; it was smaller than any of the row-boats, and had a veritable piece of common stove-pipe for a smoke-stack, which emitted a pyrotechnic column of sparks at every puff, very much like a Fourth-of-July squib. The poor man who was captain, engineer, and stoker all combined, was really so ridiculed and laughed at from our deck that he faced about and disappeared in sheer disgust at our barbarous treatment. One day only is allowed to us at Sitka, and we are told there is a great deal to see, so an end to this midnight dissipation ; we must to bed, that we may be early equipped for to-morrow.

SITKA.
(Kodak'd by Author.)

CHAPTER VIII.

FRIDAY, June 6th. — Bright and early we were up and ready to disembark. The ship, at the proper condition of the tide, had moved along to the city in the night-time, and we found ourselves, shortly after sunrise, lying at the wharf, objects of intense and welcome curiosity to the inhabitants. From my point of view, as Sitka first dawned upon me, I was instantly reminded of Naples (though of course in miniature), as I saw a group of houses nestled in the lap of the mountains on the brink of the ocean, while across the bay Mount Edgecombe bore a strong resemblance to Vesuvius. This thought I found was common to all of my fellow-passengers who had visited the Mediterranean. Mount Edgecombe is a grand specimen of an extinct volcano; and being always considerably enveloped in snow, the deep seams in its sides, furrowed by the streams of lava, which, in past years—perhaps ages—have poured from its crater, are all the more distinct and traceable. Having seen Vesuvius in full eruption, hurling high in its convulsive throes huge red-hot boulders and pouring molten lava from its lips, I could form some vague idea of the superb illumination of these hundreds of islands, their tints and lights and shadows, when the fires of this grand old mountain lit up the scene. Perhaps they will come again ; and if they do I envy those who happen to be within view. Stepping ashore, the first objects to interest us were the dilapidated warehouses at the end of the wharf, which indicated that in the olden time of Russian domination these were the busy depots where the precious cargoes of coming and going vessels were stored. (As early as 1810, the *Enterprise*, one of John Jacob Astor's ships, lay in the harbor, trading for furs with the Indians.) Just beyond these, standing upon an eminence which commands an excellent view of the town and harbor, is the Baranoff Castle, which in my opinion should be first visited in order that a clearer idea may be presently obtained of the place while you are walking through its streets. In no respect does it resemble a castle ; on the contrary, its exterior is that of a very homely country hotel. It is approached by a staircase, somewhat fatiguing in its ascent, but returning a superb view as a handsome reward for the effort. Besides, you will then be standing upon historic ground, around which cluster the scenes and incidents of the past century, with which you should make yourself familiar if you hope to appreciate what you will see when you mingle with the inhabitants. Like the island upon which it is located, the castle takes its name from that old mar-

SITKA.

tinct, the Russian Governor Baranoff, who, in the early
part of the century, fresh from his familiarity with
the horrors of Siberian life, ruled the people with a
tyranny that began with the knout and ended with the
axe.   Although it had been visited by the Russians as
early as 1741, not one of the intrepid Muscovites who
landed were left to tell the tale of capture and execu-
tion by the native Indian Sitkans.   Again, in 1799 or
1800, a party, believing themselves strong enough to
maintain their foothold, settled near here with a view of
remaining, and having placed themselves under the protection of the Archangel Gabriel, instead of stockades
and gunpowder, were in their turn also massacred and
their houses destroyed by fire.   This brought Baranoff
to the spot, who at once erected either the present or
another castle, withdrew the town from the protecting
care of Gabriel and turned it over to the Archangel
Michael.   During the latter's protectorate, it has done
better, yet it may not be out of place to mention
the fact that the spiritual guardianship has been continually supplemented by Russian bayonets and the
moral and financial, to say nothing of the physical,
power of the Shelikoff monopoly and the Hudson Bay
Company, who were the lessees of the Russian Government and controlled not only the trade but the
officials of the Archipelago.   It will be difficult to
work the imagination up to the point of believing
that this now desolate old palace was once the home
of the nobility and the scene of festivities given with
Imperial sanction and ceremony; but such is the

fact—here princes and princesses of the blood royal have eaten their caviare, quaffed their *vodhka*, and measured a minuet, surrounded by a court fresh from the palaces of St. Petersburg and Moscow. The governorship of this extreme western portion of "all the Russias" was a reward of high value, and succeeding Baranoff came a number of the nobility, each in turn provided with the revenue and retinue necessary to a proper maintenance of the dignity of his office, which appears to have chiefly consisted in luxurious and extravagant entertainment upon any pretext that should warrant it, notably the arrival of a foreign war vessel, or even a merchantman. I have had opportunity to observe how devoted these Russian nobles are to the convivial side of life, for I have been led to the banquet-room by one of the most renowned of her jolly Admirals, and have sat at table near one of her Grand Dukes whose manner indicated that for him there was but one hour in life, and that the present one; so that it was not difficult for me to picture the avidity with which in dreary Sitka they accepted any incident which would warrant them in throwing open the doors of the castle ball-room.

It was in this very house that Lady Franklin, twenty years ago spent three weeks of her aged life, (for she was then eighty years of age,) in the hope that she still might find some trace, dead or alive, of her adventurous husband, Sir John. It was here that Mr. William H. Seward, after retiring from office as Secretary of State, resided for several days, on his trip to see with his own eyes the immense territory which had been peaceably acquired for his country-

WILLIAM H. SEWARD.

men through the sagacity of himself and Senator Charles Sumner, and paid for at the rate of two cents per acre through the personal exertions of my old friend, General N. P. Banks, who was then (1867), as he is now, a member of Congress. It was from these very windows that was witnessed in the fall of 1867 a pageant of great significance to civilization, though perhaps not as splendid as others of much less consequence. In the bay on the afternoon of October the 18th lay at anchor three American war ships: the *Ossipee*, the *Resaca*, and the *Jamestown*, commanded respectively by Captains Emmons, Bradford, and McDougall, each vessel dressed in the national colors, while the Russian soldiers, citizens, and Indians of Sitka, which was then, as it is now, the capital of Alaska, had assembled upon the open space at our feet, carrying aloft the eagles of the Czar. At a given signal, the United States navy fired a national salute in honor of the Russian flag, which was then lowered from the staff upon the castle, and this salvo being responded to by the Russian garrison in compliment to ours, the stars and stripes were hoisted to the peak amidst the wild huzzas of the assembled people. Thus, five hundred and eighty thousand square miles of the earth's surface passed from the control of the most despotic monarch on the globe into the hands of the most liberal of modern governments; thus the boast of the Englishman, that the sun never sets on her Majesty's dominions, ceased to be without parallel and thus the peaceable surrender and peaceable acquisition of vast territory without resort to arms furnished an illustration which should not only commend itself to all mankind, but help to inaugurate with the coming century a universal acceptance of the new religion, that killing is murder and war is barbarism: for if statesmen here and abroad have no better occupation, for instance, than fanning a flame of irritability concerning the ownership of the unfortunate seal, who is born only to be clubbed to death, let it be left to the women, the graves of whose soldier husbands, brothers, and sons, they periodically decorate with flowers, and let it be seen whether they are not brave enough to yield a little Quixotic dignity and all the sealskin costumes they ever had or hope for, rather than again to hear the wail of woful war. We are no less patriotic than our liege lords, quite as combative I think, and just as little given to surrendering when we believe we are in the right; but we feel like the beautiful Princess Maksoutoff, who sat here at this window weeping bitter tears as the ensign of her regal master was lowered for the last time; those tears did eternal credit to her patriotism, and were doubtless a proud satisfaction and a comfort to her; but what of the tears she would have shed if, instead of seeing her husband formally yield up his authority to a friendly nation, he had been brought home to her the dead victim of a bloody strife to attain the same object.

As I looked out over this placid bay across to Mt. Edgecombe, and thence far off to the western horizon,

LINCOLN STREET, SITKA.

where the Pacific Ocean dips down to the coast of Eastern Asia, the thought came to me that over there was the birthplace, the cradle, the youth, and the manhood of civilization, and that it had journeyed and travelled westward and westward, wearied at times almost to despair, but springing up again and striking vigorous blows, sometimes in the name of religion, but oftener for conquest only, until after ages had elapsed it found its way to the western hemisphere, and in the course of time encircled the globe; and that it was now here on the confines of earth looking towards the home of its creation. I could not but contrast the joyous, healthful hour, which was ours here at the ending, with the dungeon-life of serfdom over there where it all began. "Yes, Madame," said Judge Calkins, when with some enthusiasm I gave him the benefit of this idea one evening at Tacoma, "the tail is now wagging the dog."

Descending from the Baranoff Castle and walking up the main street of the town, which was really clean and nice-looking—such a contrast to Fort Wrangell, we next became intensely interested in the Siwash Indians, who were most picturesquely grouped upon the porch of the government building, offering for sale their stock of baskets, spoons, bracelets, rings, miniature totem poles, and

(*Kodak'd by Miss M. D. Beach.*)

all kinds of knick-knacks. The prices asked were
exorbitant in the extreme, and they seemed to have
a kind of trades-union understanding among themselves that, having once fixed a price they would
adhere to it to the last. They know only two divisions
of money: a "bit," which is twelve and a half cents,
but payable with a dime; and a "dolla," dollar.
Whether they base the price upon the amount of
labor expended on each article, or whether upon the
attractiveness of it I could not tell, but it certainly was
not regulated by the supply and demand; for instance,
you would see a dozen baskets offered by a dozen
Indians, each asking three dollars as the price, whereas
you could buy for a dollar some prettier one of which
there was only a single specimen.

The Indian squaws appeared much superior to those
at Wrangell, and much better dressed, though this I discovered was owing in a great measure to the holiday
which they take upon the arrival of a ship, their attire
consisting of a full supply of female costume, fitting of
course quite loosely, of the most gaudy colors that could
be selected, bright red, green, and blue predominating,
while their ears and wrists were ornamented with a
great profusion of home-made, and in fact very well
made, gold and silver jewelry; the feet of some were
bare, others wore coarse blue worsted stockings, while
a few luxuriated in chamois-leather moccasins; the
hair was invariably brushed or oiled smoothly to the
head and plaited in the back; and each figure, young
or old, male or female, was the owner of a blanket,

which seemed as indispensable as the fan to the China-
man, or the umbrella to the Englishman, and was made
to do the service of
hood, jacket, skirt,
cushion, or lap-rug,
just as the occasion
required; generally it
hung down from the
top of the head, often
was thrown over the
shoulders, the head
being turbaned in a
highly - colored hand-
kerchief; but in the
sunshine, as they sat
selling their wares, it
was mostly brought
around the hips and
folded across the lap.

(*Kodak'd by Miss M. D. Beach.*)

It is wonderful what a superstitious aversion they
have to the camera. When we tried our Kodaks
on them they instantly enveloped themselves in their
blankets, and would not uncover until some old crone
who had an eye through a hole of her hood gave the
signal. This was in fact so mysterious that we tried
to reason with them, showed them pictures of ourselves, offered to send them their likenesses by the
next boat, but all to no purpose, and we were about
to give it up, when at the suggestion of one of
"the oldest inhabitants" we held aloft a silver dollar.

Instantly there was a change. The superstition simply
consisted in the belief that it was not healthy to do

any thing without being
paid for it, a superstition
which seems to pervade
waiters, and porters, and
chambermaids, and that
class of people all over the
world. Indeed American
civilization is doing a great
deal for the Siwash. It
reminded me of the story
told me by an officer who
accompanied Commodore
Perry's expedition to
Japan, to the effect that
when they first arrived
they could drop a five-dol-

(Kodak'd by Miss M. D. Beach.)

lar gold piece in the street and find it there the next
day, because no man but the owner would dare to lift it ;
but in a month or two the growth of American civilization had been so rapid that, at the sound of the fall of
a quarter, a dozen Japs would madly rush at it to put
foot upon it, each roundly protesting that it was his.

All along the main street of Sitka the Indian women
were assembled in little groups of four and five squatted
in the shadows of the houses, admirably counterfeiting
with their olive skins, bright black eyes, and showy
colors the Italian peasants on the steps of the churches
in Rome. Some of these women indulge in the horrid

custom, now facing into disuse I am glad to learn, of
wearing a wooden or bone or ivory button under the
lower lip, called the
labret, the shank of
which passes through a
slit made in the flesh for
this purpose; it means
nothing but adornment,
and assumes different
shapes and sizes, accord-
ing to the taste of the
wearer. Of this custom
I saw a good deal at
Wrangell, though I did
not see there what was
very conspicuous in

Sitka, namely, the use of the powder em-
bellishment, in which the Sitkan maidens
are very proficient, handling the subject *(Kodak'd by Miss M. D. Beach.)*
with a delicacy of touch which was quite remarkable,
save that the brown-berry tones of the throat, neck,
arms, and hands remained in strong contrast to the
pearly features.

Leaving these Indian men and women, who were
out in their best cloth and prettiest adornments
for the special benefit of the tourists, we now
cross the parade ground in company with Mr.
Bernhart and the commanding officer of the station,
for a visit to the rancherie, the home of these same
Siwash. Walk slowly, tread carefully, talk loudly so

THE RANCHERIE AT SITKA.

as to give notice of your coming, or send one of your
party ahead to give notice, for you are about to experience a most revolt-
ing, almost sickening
sight, and their normal
condition in costume
being bad enough, you
don't care about being
met by any sur-
prises which may
prove embarrass-
ing. *En passant*
I may say that
although in our
case every pre-
caution was taken

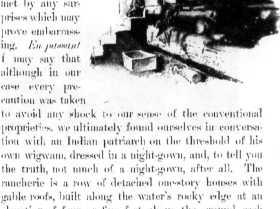

to avoid any shock to our sense of the conventional
proprieties, we ultimately found ourselves in conversation with an Indian patriarch on the threshold of his
own wigwam, dressed in a night-gown, and, to tell you
the truth, not much of a night-gown, after all. The
rancherie is a row of detached one-story houses with
gable roofs, built along the water's rocky edge at an
elevation of four or five feet above the ground, each
one approached by its separate flight of board steps.
The shore in their front is strewn confusedly with
canoes, old barrels, tin cans, clothes-lines, strings of fish
in all stages of the drying process, broken utensils, bedding set out to air, dead dogs, decaying fish and vege-
tables, and such other things as tend to excite the

olfactories (oil-factories, one of our party suggested);
—the exterior of the houses is not so bad, in fact I
doubt whether the fishermen on the North Atlantic
coast have any better, yet this makes the filth of the
inhabitants and their miserable methods the more ob-
servable. Each family seems to have as many dogs as
children: the former are a mangy, mongrel breed of

Esquimaux, and the latter, poor things, are, for the
most part, blind, deformed in limb, crippled, and nearly
all tainted with marks of scrofula. The able-bodied
men were off on their fishing expeditions, or employed
at the salmon canneries along the coast; the young
squaws ran around bare-footed and bare-legged, and the
older people of both sexes seemed to have nothing to
do but sit around the fire.

We went first to the house of the far-famed and very
rich Princess Thom, who is said to be worth $100,000

(though we saw little evidence of any such luxurious
wealth), which she has acquired through shrewd trading with her own race and the white folk. Her adopted
name is Emaline Baker, and she resides at house number 6,700 of the rancherie. During the administration of
Captain Beardslee, of the U. S. Navy, in 1879 all the
houses of the Indians were numbered; and for some very
good reason no doubt, which was not explained to me, to
each number are added two cyphers, so that the home of
the Princess was in reality No. 67, though the four figures over the door read 6,700. Her Royal Highness was
hardly ready to receive at this early hour of the morning,
as was evidenced by her bare feet, which we afterwards
saw daintily shod as she sat with her subjects on the steps
of the Government House, but they were as clean as
though just from the Russian bath around the corner,
and she welcomed us with the same
obsequious politeness with
which the Chatham Street
clothier would ask " Don't
you want to buy a nice
coat?" She is very
fat, of course not
very fair, and much
over forty, and
when we entered
the palace offered
us chairs while she
went for the arti-
cles of *bijouterie*

PRINCESS THOM.
(Kodak'd by Miss M. D. Beach.)

and *certa*, which she desired to exchange for coin (they
do not take greenbacks, are not predisposed towards gold,
but are all in favor of unlimited silver). These consisted
of bracelets, bangles, earrings, baskets, and wood carvings, very beautifully made by her people, upon which
she had advanced money during the winter, from her sur-
plus in the treasury. The palace itself, like all the houses
in the row, had one large room and a small annex in
the rear, the customary fire in the centre, and her regal
couch was not only quite a comfortable bedstead, but
the bedding, blankets, and sheets were all neat and
clean. Her "man of
equal rights" was also
present; whether he was
a prince I really cannot
say—he didn't look it :
he was much younger
than the Princess, but as
he was her seventeenth
husband it is fair to
presume that the stock
of marriageable older
ones had run out. Two
doors beyond the home
of the Princess (at No.

(*Kodak'd by Miss M. B. Roach.*)

6,900) is that of a religious fanatic over whose door is
a sign upon which are painted the words, "Elisha
Ltahin—head of a large family of orthodox Christians."

If all the homes had been as orderly and well kept
as the Princess Thom's there would have been little

INTERIOR OF INDIAN'S HOUSE AT SITKA.

to excite disgust, but they were far from it. I entered
one or two others which I was told were fair samples
of all, and was horrified at what I was compelled to see.
In the corner of one sat an old man totally blind and
idiotic, a young woman squatted at the fire cooking
some horrid greasy stuff that looked like tallow, a
middle-aged stupid-looking squaw and her child both
wrapped in their blankets sitting on the floor waiting
for the morning meal, a squalid unwashed baby scream-
ing from another corner, and two or three stalwart, lazy
men lounging around with their hands in their pockets;
encircling the room was an elevated platform upon
which were thrown, not with the artistic indifference
to arrangement recommended by Oscar Wilde, but in a
confused mass, without any other rule than to find a
place for them, every imaginable thing that these people had been able to procure by buying or begging,
from a broken clock to a bandbox. Here was a rude
bedstead, made of plank and covered with a mass of hay
or sea-weed, or something of that sort; alongside of it
a clothes-line, from which the sleeper inhaled the
moisture from the half-washed clothes; on the wall at
the bedside, wearing apparel in all stages of decay,
covered with dust and splashed with mud; cans of oil
and paint, baskets of potatoes, nets and ropes reeking
with the odor of decomposed fish, pots and kettles,
wardrobes, flour-barrels and soap-boxes; and from the
rafters hung smoked salmon and bits of bacon and
fresh meat. The odors were simply frightful, and
though I did not count how many distinct smells I

perceived, I shall ever feel grateful to the giddy, be-jewelled squaw who entered as I was taking my leave, and gave me the benefit of an aroma of musk which for the first time in my life I found most useful and refreshing.

Passing along and edging our way nervously through the pack of half-starved dogs which infest the neighborhood as they do the slums of Constantinople and Amsterdam, we came to the old man in his *robe de nuit*. If we had any inclination to laugh it was soon dispelled. Poor creature! he was emaciated, paralyzed, and, I think, demented; and in the midst of his jabbering and solicitations that we would enter his cabin, we dropped a coin into his claw-like hand and passed on. And just here I saw a dog which I shall remember all my life; he was a weird and phantom dog, large, and originally white, but his coat was falling off, exposing spots of bright pink skin; in canine language he had the mange, and he sat on his hind legs a shivering, pitiful, miserable thing that it would have been a mercy to shoot, though this doubt-less would have brought down upon us the rage of the entire rancherie. The South American poet intended to describe that creature when he said, "*No era una perra sarnosa, era una sarna perrosa.*" I had seen enough, more than I care to tell, and I retraced my steps through the throng of men, women, children, and dogs, all dirty, infected, diseased, and most miserable. Dante's famous line best expresses our feelings: "*Non ragionam di lai, ma guarda e passa.*"

We next visited the shops kept by Americans, who had a much larger and choicer assortment of curios than the Indians, among them a quaint, unique Russian samovar, some totems carved on walrus ivory handsomely inlaid with pebbles, many remarkable bits of Indian carving, and hundreds of prettily shaped and brilliantly decorated baskets. Next we found ourselves with a crowd of our fellow-passengers in another shop, buying photographic views of Alaska from the cameras of Tabor, of San Francisco, and Partridge, of Portland; they were quite cheap, and much better than I saw anywhere else; so I recommend you, if you desire to make a collection, to do it here, as you will not have such another opportunity.

At the head of the main street of Sitka and at right angles to it is the Russo-Greek Church of Saint

Michael, laid out, of course, in the form of the Greek cross, and following in every particular the architectural design of similar edifices in the mother country. It seems incongruous and out of place in a little town like Sitka, though in the courtly days of Baranoff, and Kupreanoff, and Maksoutoff, and all the other "offs," it was an indispensable adjunct to the state pageantry of the pe-

GREEK CHURCH AT SITKA.
(Kodak'd by Author.)

riod. The porch or entrance is surmounted by a
square tower of two stories, upon which is a belfry
containing a chime of several bells, and above, a very
symmetrical radish-shaped spire (excuse the simile),
topped by a cross of four distinct crosses ; over the
nave is a Byzantine dome, and above this a cupola
again surmounted by the compound Greek cross. The
dome and spire were once painted green, and the crosses
gilded, but the rains and fogs of the Alaskan coast
have destroyed the brilliancy of these colors, and to-
day, like all else that is ancient and historical in
Sitka, they are "sicklied o'er with the pale cast" of
neglect.

The arrival of Archbishop Vladimir was quite an
event at Sitka. He is the prelate of his Church in America, and it soon became known that at eleven o'clock
he would hold a special service. At that hour there
was assembled beneath the dome a very remarkable
congregation—a *melange* of Indians, Russians, Americans, and sailors and tourists from our ship. We stood up
during the entire service, there being no seats. Archbishop Vladimir and his four assistants wore the sacer-
dotal ornaments of their respective offices, which were
really superb ; the garments were of exquisite texture
of gold, silver, and silk embroidery, and the mitres
studded with rare jewels of, I should think, immense
value. The liturgy, in the Slavonic language, was
chanted by one of the priests, who had the most musical bass voice I ever heard (though aboard ship he
smoked cigarettes from morning until night), and by a

choir of Indian boys. Taking it all in all, the service was most impressive; the native children, Russian and Indian, well dressed and genteel-looking, seeming to thoroughly comprehend what was going on, were continually bowing the head and making the sign of the cross; they were scholars in the church school. At the conclusion of the ritual the Archbishop delivered an address, and as he turned his face towards us I realized the truth of what I had somewhere read about the Greek Church and its priesthood, to the effect that the prelates are selected from among the bishops, who are all celibates, and that the preference falls upon those whose features most resemble the traditional Christ. Archbishop Vladimir, as a passenger on the good ship *Queen*, was a very tall, rather thin man, clad in a long cloak to his ankles and a cape to his elbows, and wearing a very broad-brimmed, low-crowned felt hat, his hair being plaited and tied in a little bunch at his neck. At the altar, dressed in the purple and gold robes of his Church, he had a face of amiable benevolence, a soft, flossy moustache and beard, his hair parted in the centre and flowing gracefully over his shoulders. The carefully studied imitation was apparent on the instant; there you saw the ideal picture in the centre of Leonardo da Vinci's fresco of "The Last Supper." I wish with all my heart I could have comprehended his words, for I could see by his gestures that they were earnest, simple, instructive, and loving. The service being over, he came down among his people, laying hands upon them and blessing them with a smile so full of tenderness that I am sure every lowly, ragged Indian who kissed his hand was a little better for the contact, though I should have been very sorry to have submitted mine to the same experience.

While this was going on I availed myself of the confusion incident to the crowding around the Archbishop to take a look at the interior treasures and decorations of the church, which are a great surprise measured by the impression made by the fading colors and apparent neglect of the exterior. There are two altars in the transepts, the larger one being shut off excepting during the service by two golden bronze doors, each exquisitely ornamented by solid silver images of the patron saints, the doors themselves being of fretted and open work and most effective pattern. All the panels are decorated by oil paintings, the details of which are executed with the care of the miniature painter, and bear the very closest scrutiny. Many of these are framed, as it were, with silver, the drapery and ornaments of the body being of that metal, while the features, hands, and feet are in colors,—a quaint combination, yet very effective. They gave the impression of being the work of a master-hand, and I much regretted that there appeared to be no means of ascertaining the artist's name. An hour can be very well spent here by the art student.

Among those present during the entire service I observed two very charming young women, who were evidently as little a part of what was going on as I was myself, and with them a lovely blue-eyed child of about three years of age, whose pure white skin and pretty dress made him a beautiful pearl among the tawny skins of the unwashed natives. After a little hesitation, I approached and introduced myself, only to discover that they were just as anxious to speak with me as I was to talk with them. Of course it resulted in our becoming fast friends for the remainder of the day, as they proved to be the wives of officers of the *Pinta*, which vessel, you will remember, we left at Fort Wrangell. One of them, Mrs. F., was from Philadelphia, the city of "homes"; the other, Mrs. K., from Washington, the city of "social life"; and here they were out on the far-off coast of Alaska, and had been for ever so long, without either home or society. One of them resided in apartments at a restaurant or tavern near the church, which her own taste and familiarity with refinement had made habitable, and the other (whose husband happened to be with her) lived over a shop across the street in a couple of rooms approached over a creaky, tumble-down staircase, but rather cosey when you got into them and experienced the hospitality of the pleasant hostess. Nevertheless they seemed happy, at least they would not confess that they were not so; still, I made a vow, on the spot, that if I am ever a widow, naval officers need not apply. Said one of them: "I expect to leave this place in September, but have no idea where we will be ordered." Said the other: "I have been here three years—my boy is a Sitkan." Now Sitka is very beautiful, very romantic, is getting to be a good deal talked of all over the world, and will probably grow and prosper, but it is no place for charming young women to spend three or four of the best years of their young lives, separated from their husbands most of that time, and left almost entirely to the uncongenial society of a population seven eighths of whom belong to the race who twice in the history of the city have massacred the whites. These ladies confessed to me that there was no diversion or amusement whatever at this post, excepting "just a little scandal and a good deal of poker," and that even this grew monotonous and had to be varied with fishing and hunting, and there the excitement ended, excepting on steamer days, which was really the only event which dispelled their *ennui*. They depend entirely upon the Russians for domestic servants, and these are not only very independent, but troublesome in many other ways.

We learned here that every thing American, which the Indians think well of, they call "Boston"; those who are Americanized call themselves "Boston Siwashes"; the missionaries are known as "Boston men," and the steamers as "Boston ships"; and this brought from a fellow-passenger a capital story which may be old, but was not so to me, and would be given here even though I were a Boston woman myself. It is of a patriotic young girl from the "Hub" who, being asked to account for there being so much larger a proportion of Unitarians in Boston than in any other city in the world, replied : "I suppose it is because we cannot bring ourselves to subscribe to the doctrine of regeneration, for who, being born in Boston, would have any desire or occasion to be born again."

Hearing that the Indian River in the suburbs of the town is worthy of a visit, we accepted the escort of our two young friends, and after a walk of half a mile (I believe I have already said that there are few horses in Alaska, and no carriages) we came to a really very quaint and romantic lane, leading to a clear and rapid stream over which is thrown a pretty rustic suspension bridge. It is a very charming spot, rich with ferns of most delicate texture and brightest green and velvet mosses, such as those which border the footpaths through the woods in England, a bower of wild foliage in fact, of exquisite color. By all means stroll through it, if for no other purpose than to inhale the pure air that has never come in contact with the rancherie. On your way back, you will discover, per-

THE INDIAN RIVER WALK AT SITKA.

haps, that Alaska, like Ireland, has her "blarney-stone," but why, I really cannot tell, for, excepting the little group of my own countrywomen, who might be counted on the fingers, there is not another face in Sitka which would reflect a responsive smile to the sweetest thing that fell from lips that had kissed the blarney-stone a hundred times. The stone may be recognized, should you have any difficulty in finding it, by the names of tourists and inscriptions cut all over it in all the tongues of the Tower of Babel.

And now, quite by accident, I had perhaps the most interesting experience of my whole trip,——certainly one that has made an everlasting impression upon my mind : an object lesson which often and often will set me thinking, a subject which would require a volume to do it approximate justice. The joyous shouting of half a hundred boys, some of them dashing across the road in

pursuit of a foot-ball; well-clothed, well-fed boys; healthy, vigorous, intelligent boys ; Indians, half-breeds, Musco-vites, and a few Americans. What did it mean ? From where had they so suddenly come ? From school.

These were the beneficiaries of the "Presbyterian
Board of Home Missions," and the large building on
the right of the road is the school-house. Of course I
had read about this Mission; all the books on Alaska
refer to it more or less; yet the knowledge of its existence had brought no special desire to visit the place.
To me Sitka was the vestige of a departed empire;
the home of a decaying race of aborigines; a depot for
the sale of Russo-Indian relics and curios; a pretty
little town timidly hiding away in among the mountains; and for that I had come to see it and had been
amply repaid. But the "Mission" I had never thought
of; perhaps the book-writers had failed to attract me to
it; perhaps my faith in missions generally was not very
confirmed; perhaps I did not believe what I read about
them. Be that as it may, hereafter no man, nor woman
either, shall outdo me in words of praise and thanks
for the glorious Godlike work which is being performed
by the good people who are rescuing the lives, the
bodies, and the souls of these poor creatures from the
physical and moral deaths they are dying. I am not a
Christian woman; my faith is that of the chosen people who were led out of Egyptian tyranny and darkness by the pillar of fire and the pillar of cloud; but
my whole nature is in accord with these Christian men
and women, whose immolation and sacrifices to regen-
erate their fellow-creatures will surely meet with
heavenly reward, no matter what their creed. I wish
I had had more time at my disposal to spend with the
teachers and the scholars so that I might now give

even a skeleton outline of their daily life; but I may
say to those who desire to know more than my brief
acquaintance with the subject enables me to tell them,
that these Mission schools of Alaska are in charge of
the Rev. Sheldon Jackson, whose address is Sitka, and
although I had not the pleasure of meeting him (as he
was absent), I am sure he will most cheerfully give
any information asked for. The Rev. A. E. Austin and
Mrs. Austin, having observed our party entering the
school-house grounds, received us at the door, and from
that moment until the blowing of the ship's whistle
admonished us that we must leave them, were exceedingly kind and polite, facilitating our inspection of the
school in such a systematic way that we were really
able to gather much information in addition to experiencing a most novel and enjoyable visit.

There are about one hundred boys and fifty girls in
the institution, some of them being only three years of

MRS. SHEPARD'S TRAINING-SCHOOL.
(*Kodak'd by Author.*)

age and others as old as
twenty-two. The scholastic
education is very properly
confined entirely to the English branches; but this is supplemented by the training-
schools, founded and maintained by Mrs. Elliott F.
Shepard, of New York, where
the boys are instructed in
carpentry, shoemaking, and
black-smithing, and the girls

are taught dress-making and the use of the sewing-machine. I went first into one of the class-rooms of the
males, where I saw perhaps twenty dark-skinned Siwash
Indian boys, whose Mongolian faces and almond-shaped
eyes had assumed an expression of intelligence, so different from the stupid, blear-eyed appearance of the same
age and race whom I had seen in the rancherie, that it
was difficult to realize that they could possibly be twigs
of the same tree. Two of the boys were at the black-
board working out a sum in Algebra (a thing I couldn't
do myself for the life of me); and here we lingered
for a few minutes while Mrs. John H. DeVore, of Corry,
Pennsylvania, the teacher of the class, gave us a fair
sample of the progress being made by her pupils.
Next we went to the Primary Department over which
Miss Delph of Crestline, Ohio, presided, who, with
great patience and kindly forbearance, was performing
the difficult operation of extracting the guttural sounds
from two Indian maidens' throats and adapting them
to the pronunciation of English words. Up-stairs we

found the dormitories,
like every thing else
about the establishment,
orderly, neat, and clean,
due regard being paid to
the number allotted to
each room, and to the
subject of heating and
ventilation. In the sew-
ing department were

THE MISSION CHILDREN.
(*Kodak'd by Author.*)

several girls operating skilfully upon the sewing-machine, others cutting from the piece, and younger ones basting for the sewing girls. The colors of the material were all bright, in fact quite gaudy, giving proof that these children are encouraged to gratify the harmless tastes of their race, which is eminently proper.

Next we were taken to Mrs. Shepard's shops, and although the work was over for the day, we could plainly see by the specimens of handiwork all around us what a noble charity her philanthropy and bounty had created. Every thing within sight of us had been built by the Indian boys who were the pupils of the Presbyterian Mission and of Mrs. Shepard's training-school, including the school-houses themselves, (for they had recently been destroyed by fire,) and the group of little cottages in the distance which Mrs. Austin begs us to visit, that we may have an opportunity of seeing "how our pupils live when they marry and go to housekeeping." "Joseph" was at home when we knocked at the door, but his wife and little ones had gone down to the landing to see the new ship (the *Queen*). Joseph was a man of about twenty-five years of age I should say ; when we disturbed him he was sitting at a table in his little parlor writing a letter which I saw commenced "My dearest and best friend," It was being written to a Mr. Miller in the East, who had been his benefactor and to whom he chiefly owed his rescue from a life of idleness or worse. Joseph was living in a house which he had built himself, every inch of it, doors, windows, staircases, tables, every

thing in fact that a carpenter could make, was the work
of his own hands. His parlor was a perfect gem of
taste, order and cleanliness, and as for his two bed-
rooms on the second story, which we all visited (a
dozen or more of us) they couldn't have been sweeter
or neater if they had been placed there purposely for
exhibition. My only regret was that I had not the
opportunity of seeing the woman whose innate and
once latent sense of refinement had been developed by
the instruction she had received in the Mission school,
for no other kind of woman could have spread those
little comforts of the toilet so daintily on the bureau, or
decorated the walls so picturesquely and tastefully
with photographs and prints.

Attached to the school are two hospitals also en-
dowed by Mrs. Shepard, but neither of them having
many patients. In one was a little consumptive child,
doomed no doubt to an early death; one of those un-
fortunates who suffer "for the sins of the fathers to
the third and fourth generation": another was a
rheumatic, whose neglected infancy had destroyed a
life that could now, through the beneficence of education, be made happy and useful had not her health
been undermined in the damp pits of the rancherie.
A third was a sufferer from ophthalmia, produced
perhaps by lack of cleanliness and living in an atmosphere of smoke.

It is said somewhere that it is only a single step
from civilization to barbarism,—perhaps so. If all
wrongdoing is barbaric, the saying is not only trite

but true, for a false civilization often begets the very
worst of crimes. But I and those ladies and gentlemen who accompanied me through the rancherie and
the schools at Sitka can vouch for the fact that it
is only half a mile from savage, uncivilized ignorance,
superstition, filth, and immorality, to education, de-
portment, thrift, domestic felicity, and all human
happiness. Thank God I had seen "*le revers de la
medaille.*" To have gone back to my comfortable
home in New York and to the embraces of my bright,
healthy, intelligent children, feeling that these poor
little wretches at Sitka were to remain outcasts during
the brief time that disease and degradation should permit
them to exist on earth, would have been a great sorrow.
Thanks to the Presbyterian Board of Home Missions
and to Mrs. Elliott F. Shepard, the reverse is a great joy.

THE MUSEUM AT SITKA.
(*Kodak'd by Author.*)

CHAPTER IX.

AS the time arrived for our departure from Sitka a great portion of the population came down to the landing, and just before we started we were surprised to see approaching the ship a long procession headed by a brass band which played quite good music. These were some of the pupils from the Mission school, and the musicians were Indian boys from the school also. Arrived at the landing they formed an interesting group, at which we all levelled our Kodaks, much to the amusement of the youngsters, who, no doubt, thought some of us a little crazy; the hat was passed around, and the band added about thirty dollars to its fund for new instruments. When we finally began to move away, we received rs affec-

(Kodak'd by Author.)

tionate and regretful an adieu from the crowded wharf
as though the spectators were parting with their nearest
kin. The young American women waved their handkerchief; the men shouted their cheers, and the little
Siwash tots kissed their hands till we were too far
away to distinguish their forms as they took a last
fond lingering look at the dissolving view of the ship.

And, oh, what a charming picture was ours as we
steamed out of the harbor of Sitka at six o'clock that
lovely summer evening! The sky could not have been
a more cloudless azure blue; it was just cool enough
to provoke a walk to and
fro upon the deck; there
was so little air stirring
that the smoke ascended
in a perpendicular column
from the stack, and the
sheen upon the water made
the ocean a sea of sil-
ver. We all felt so
jolly; everybody de-
lighted with the day's
experience, and each
person having some lit-
tle episode to relate of
the day spent in Sitka.
Not a grumbler; not a
single soul disappoint-
ed about the slight-
est thing; in fact it

(Kodak'd by Author.)

was my first experience in my many voyages of pleasure, where universal satisfaction was the result of the day's experience. Yet I could not help thinking of the desolation to which our departure condemned those who had been so kind to us; nor of those poor souls whose darkness may never be dispelled by the enlightenment of education and civilization; and it occurred to me that if I owned the steamship line I would build a little hotel there, that the passengers might have an opportunity of occupying a week in excursions to points of interest, which it is impossible to reach in a large ship, and then life at Sitka would not be so intolerable; and that if I was the government of the United States, I would put the Indians under such discipline that their quarters should be subject to inspection, and their children compelled to go to school. What two great boons these would be to Sitka, and how easy to accomplish both. But the scenery is so beautifully grand that I must keep my moralizing for some future time.

This is the Sitkan Archipelago, and we are in the midst of so many islands that I don't know whether to speak of them by hundreds or thousands; they are exquisite emerald, pink, yellow, and crimson islands all of them, so close to each other that the deer swim to and fro as the canary leaps from perch to perch, and the shadows of their tall forests fall from one to the other just as the housetop throws its shade across the street; yet the channel is so deep between them that we circle and wind in and out of them at a rate of speed which

throws the water high up upon their banks, frighten-
ing the wild ducks and geese, who in flocks and
couples dart across our bow continually.   Mount
Edgecombe, five miles right ahead of us, becomes
the centre of observation and the subject of conversation.   Every field-glass on the ship is levelled
at it, and we distinctly see the gaping mouth of the
crater and the deep ravines cut by the rivers of
lava which have rolled to its base.   We again take
the outer channel, keeping Mount Edgecombe on our
right for several hours, it appeared to me,—each view
of it being more and more confirmatory of its volcanic
character.   We are now passing around Kruzof Island,
and when well out to sea, steer due north along the
western coast of Tchitchagoff Island towards Cross
Sound, which is the outlet of Glacier Bay.   It is half-
past ten o'clock when we approach Cape Cross, yet it
is daylight, real daylight, by which you can read a
newspaper just as well as at tea-time.   What is that
white streak above the horizon right ahead of us?   Is
it a cloud, or some optical illusion?   "Nothing of the
kind; it is the Fairweather range, the most beautiful
snow mountains in the world," says Captain Carroll.
"Sorry it will be a l   dark when we get there, but
you shall see the   .aylight if the weather holds
up."   Fortunate.   .s we were out of reach of tele-
graphic communication, the Weather Bureau had no
chance to dash our hopes with prognostications of
"cloudy, followed by local rains," or any nonsense of
that kind, and as the sun had gone down full of

promise, we had every reason to feel hopeful that the Captain would be able to keep his word, and well did he keep it two days later.

But, to return to Cross Sound; by reference to the maps you will find that here we change our course abruptly to the right, and you will also remark, probably, that this water is called on some of them

Icy Strait. It is eleven o'clock; hardly a passenger has retired for the night—night, did I say? Night it may have been by the clock, but by the heavens it was a night of continual day. Some of us had determined not to go to bed at all, and the Captain, overhearing this heroic resolve, promptly placed both kitchen and pantry at our disposal, and joined our party, amiably giving us the names of the mountains,

capes, and islands as we approached them. I knew
not how often, if ever, the scene before me had
been viewed to such advantage by others, but, for
myself, I felt the inspiration of the hour so profoundly
that I could scarce believe it was part of that same
earth which I had left behind me but a few brief days.
In a group of a dozen or twenty people among whom
I stood there were periods of several minutes, I
should think, when not a word was uttered, except,
perhaps, a half-suppressed exclamation of awe and
admiration. For my part, I leaned upon the rail of
the ship, peering into the twilight, every now and then
catching a glimpse of some new wonder in the distance
and trying to mould it into form; filled with an ecstasy
of amazement and surprise which I had never before
experienced in a somewhat adventurous life. Along
the horizon, in a complete semicircle from left to right,
was a streak of golden fire—that kind of molten, liquid
fire which pours from the blast-furnace in the night-
time and courses its way through the gutters made to
receive it in the clay,—and where the snow mountains
broke in upon its lines, it lit them up with tints of the
most delicate pink, just soft enough to mark their outlines against the gray-green twilight beyond. And
the shades of this twilight, how beautiful and delicate
in color were they! from the deep blue which bordered
the golden horizon, through all the color varieties of
the aurora borealis to the faintest touch of amber and
almost invisible green, yet all lit up with the still
lingering beams of the now far-distant sun; while

away off in the northwest, suspended, as it were, like a bright electric light, over the coast of Asia was a single planet (I know not which) struggling in her silvery purity for a place in this superb panorama where none of her lesser sisters dared to venture. In this surprising effect of light and shade, nature gave us a wonderful example of what is called in art *la magie du coloris*. And thus for three or four hours did one day resolve itself into another, without the intermediate night. Those who went to bed left word with friends to call them when there was any change of scene or incident; others dozed in the social hall, fearing to trust themselves to sounder sleep: while many had their chairs and blankets brought on deck, where at intervals they refreshed themselves with hot coffee abundantly supplied by the obliging stewards.

It was the "dawn of the morning" on Saturday, June 7th, when we first saw floating ice; a piece about the size of a row-boat and about the same shape, but it was large enough to serve as a signal

(*Kodak'd by Miss Margaret Watson.*)

to awaken the sleepers, so that in a few minutes the deck was peopled with a motley crowd, in all kinds of incomplete costume, from a shawl and skirt to a water proof and a pair of rubbers; we hurriedly

got down to our normal condition however, and in a
little while, everybody was on deck attired for the
day, and before the sun rose we had passed within view
a glacier on our left, which in the distance resembled a
river suddenly frozen and held in solidity by the vise-
grip of two lofty mountains.   Rounding the cape and
parting company with the beautiful Fairweather Mountains, we are now in Glacier Bay steering directly north,
with the Beardslee cluster of picturesque islands on
our right and straggling icebergs all around us.   Ahead
of us, in the distance, is Willoughby Island, and our
straightest course to the Muir Glacier would leave this
island on the left, but there are two or three very interesting glaciers on the west coast of Glacier Bay
which Captain Carroll, with characteristic courtesy, is
anxious we should see, so he makes for the narrow
channel between the island and the western shore.   It
was seven o'clock in the morning when we entered this
passage, which I should judge was perhaps half a mile
wide and four miles in length, but we found it so

densely packed with icebergs
and floating ice, that we did
not extricate ourselves from
it until noon; in other words,
our progress was at the rate of
about one mile an hour. Those
five hours were full of intense
interest and excitement and
sometimes of anxiety.   I do
no injustice to Captain Carroll

(Kodak'd by Author.)

when I venture the belief that if he had known the real condition of the channel he would have taken the easterly course; at all events it was patent to every one on board, from the prudence with which the ship was handled and the precautions which were taken to avert any too violent collision with the huge floating masses which confronted us, that the occasion was an extraordinary one. These icebergs were curious studies; I did not fail to realize that each one of them outranked in age any other moving thing I had ever seen, save perhaps the moon. For hundreds of years these tons and tons of solid ice have been slowly forcing their way down to the temperate waters of the North Pacific Ocean, bearing upon their begrimed sides and edges the evidence of fierce struggles for freedom with the rock-bound passes in the mountains, and carrying victoriously aloft the massive granite slabs and boulders crunched in the conflict. Thicker and thicker grew the sea of ice, larger and more threatening the bergs, many of them rising to the level of our upper deck and grazing the ship's side as we slowly forged ahead. The atmosphere too grew thick and threatening, and I overheard the Captain mutter, " Pretty place to be caught in a fog," as he peered anxiously ahead through his glasses. Fortunately I had unlimited and not misplaced confidence in his seamanship, otherwise I should have missed the exhilarating sensation with which the novel surroundings filled me.

For the first time on the trip, it became quite cold and damp—overcoats and wraps were in demand,

and those of us who were fortunate enough to find room upon the platform in rear of the bridge, were treated to as beautiful a specimen of skilful ship steering as can be imagined. The Captain had been at his post from the time we left Sitka on the previous evening, still he showed no sign of fatigue; on the contrary, his head and eye must both have been uncommonly clear to have brought so large an ocean ship through such a field of obstacles without the slightest accident. I know, for he told me so, that he fully expected to lose one, or perhaps two, blades of the propeller, and I could see by the contortions of his face as we thumped against a hundred tons of floating ice and topped it over bottom up, that he was not quite sure of the result when the great ungainly mass swung back again toward the ship. Constantly these bergs, as they split in half under the prow of the steamer, rolled over and exposed the red paint, which too plainly told of blows of sharp contact with our keel, much to the chagrin of Captain Carroll, who avowed he had not come there "to paint Glacier Bay red"; in fact, he chafed at every chafe. I learned that it was of great importance to keep the ship constantly moving ahead, even though her advance could be measured only by inches, so that I continually turned my eyes to some tree or rock upon the shore to judge by this fixed object whether we were making progress, for the current was carrying the ice so fast past us that it was impossible to judge whether the apparent headway of the vessel was not after all an illusion. Once, and only once, we came to a dead stop; the surface of the water could be nowhere seen; the narrow channel was itself a glacier, and the crunching masses of huge slabs of marble ice which choked it piled themselves one upon the other, like sheep driven into a *cul-de-sac*. It was a moment of some anxiety.

The men seemed to realize the peril more than the women, for they had been interviewing the sailors and had learned that no such ice-flow had been encountered since Captain Carroll first explored these waters seven years before. We women did not at the moment comprehend that the contact of the propeller with one of these bergs

(*Kodak'd by Author.*)

might render the ship entirely helpless in a place beyond the reach of succor, and in a sea which would pulverize our little steam launch if we attempted to use her, so that we were deprived even of the ability to search for assistance in case of need. Presently, however, there was a gentle movement of the machinery, a little commotion among the icebergs in our rear, a grating and a scraping sound which was echoed over the entire field by the crackling of the disintegrating ice, and looking again at my landmark on the shore, I found we were once more pushing forward. At one time the Captain ran half-way up the foremast, glasses in hand, and for some minutes, like the picture of

Farragut in Mobile Bay, shouted his orders to the wheel-house. Then again resuming his monotonous and nervous pacing upon the bridge from port to starboard and starboard to port, he steered his immense vessel with such dexterity and mathematical precision that as the cakes of ice were upturned and fell gracefully into our wake, it was easy to see that the course he selected was the one of least resistance. I took note of a few of the expressions whose magnetic influence twisted and turned us around in such beautiful curves, some of which were: "Starboard, sir!" "Slow her!" "Why don't he slow her when I tell him!" "Stop her!" "Go tell that engineer if he don't obey the signals quicker, the first thing he knows he'll have one of these bergs in his engine-room!" "Hard-a-port, sir!" "Port her!" "Steady now!" "Keep your eye on the compass there!" "Put an extra man at the wheel!" and so on, doubtless conveying to the persons for whom they were intended volumes of instruction, but to me nothing but the sense of security with which his general watchfulness inspired me.

In the midst of all this strain, when perhaps the slightest error of judgment might have been fraught with disaster, the chief steward (it was his first voyage with Captain Carroll) was seen ascending the ladder with a bowl of nice hot, steaming coffee for our able commander, who at that moment was the cynosure of every eye. I am sure everybody felt proud of that steward; wanted to shake him by the hand; was grateful to him; wondered why they hadn't thought of it themselves. "I've brought you a cup of coffee," mildly whispered the steward, with outstretched hand. "Take it away, sir! When I want coffee I'll send for it," shouted the skipper. What became of the steward I don't know; but I do know that there were a few disjointed scraps of sentences floating around the atmosphere for several minutes, such as: "Nice time for coffee!—Port her!—Steady!—Pretty time to be drinking coffee!—Starboard a little!—Coffee, indeed!—Slow her, sir!—Slow her, I say!—Coffee!" It is proper to say, however, that a few hours later the poor affrighted steward was addressed in language as courtly as: "I'll take that coffee now, steward, but don't ever bother me again when I've got my hands full."

Of course it is very difficult to convey by words any appreciable or intelligent idea of the scene through which we were passing, nor can I hope to do so fully by the aid of my camera; for I find that where the ice was densest the atmosphere was too thick to secure prints which would bear reproduction; still, those which I obtained, when the fog lifted in spots which were less obstructed, may perhaps serve the purpose measurably. I can only say that, as far as the eye could reach in all directions, the ocean was covered with masses of ice, varying in size from that of a large house to that of the morning supply at the area gate after a mild winter; and they were of all imaginable shapes—many containing deep caverns with stalactite roofs; many honey-combed

through and through like huge white coral; some
assuming the forms of Indian tents, churches, stables,
and ships; not fantastic creations, but so marked as
to attract the attention of the whole ship's company.
But the coloring was even more remarkable, the pre-
vailing tint being that exquisite blue of which the
turquoise is perhaps the only specimen, spotted here
and there and sometimes half clothed with a covering
of sparkling snow.

When at last, after much tribulation, we once
more reached the open sea between Willoughby
Island and the entrance to Muir Inlet, for miles along
the beach of Scidmore Island were stranded a chain
of these exquisite turquoise gems which excited
our admiration to the highest pitch. Far over to the
left were the three glaciers in whose honor we had
passed through this sea of troubles, but so choked
were the approaches to them that a telescopic view
was all we had, yet this of itself was worth coming
for; while far off towards the horizon on the right
were clustered together a squadron of floating pyramids, whose white sides and uniformity of shape
brought vividly to mind the regatta scenes of Newport
and New London, where for hours the fleet remains
at anchor waiting for the wind. We are now at the
mouth of Muir Inlet: the great glacier is in front of
us, but only in faint outline as yet; the lunch bell has
sounded, and we are told that before the meal is finished we will be at anchor within the shadow of this
world's wonder. So to lunch we go, and while I am

there, you, my daughter, may familiarize yourself as I did with what has already been written of it, which, to save you much trouble and research, I will epitomize as follows : The Muir Glacier is situate at the head of Glacier Bay about eight hundred miles from Tacoma, our starting point. It is one of many outlets of the enormous field of glacial ice which stellates from a centre about fifteen miles back of the Muir front, and covers the valleys of the yet unexplored mountains between the Pacific Ocean and the head-waters of the great Yukon River (said to be the largest river on the globe). The area which the glacier covers is as yet unknown, though beyond doubt the human eye can follow it for a distance of forty miles, look across it fifteen miles, and has located sixteen other lesser glaciers which are tributary to it. It derives its name very properly from Prof. John Muir, the State Geologist of California, who, as far as is known, was the first white man to visit it; Vancouver and the early navigators and explorers, although familiar with the enormous outflow of ice, not having had the intrepidity or perhaps the equipment necessary to penetrate beyond the entrance to the bay (Captain James Carroll, now of the *Queen*, but in 1883 commanding the *Idaho*, being the first seaman to approach within reasonable distance and come to anchor within full view of it). In fact, it is only eleven years ago (1879) since Professor Muir first saw it from an Indian canoe, and it is exceedingly doubtful whether five thousand white people all told have *ever* seen it, though I have little doubt that a

greater number than that will visit it annually hereafter, the trouble of getting there being reduced to a
luxury, and the result more delightful than that which
has ever yet rewarded the searcher for the beautiful
and wonderful in nature.

The walls which bound the Muir Glacier on either
side vary in height from three thousand two hundred to five thousand feet above the level of the
ice, and where the slow-moving mass emerges from
the jaws of this vise of rock, the glacier is three
miles in width and five hundred feet above the
level of the bay, but from this point down towards
the water it narrows its width until, at the water-
front, it becomes clogged between the barren moraines
which it itself has created, and finds its passage to the
sea limited to a front of just one mile. Its façade at
this point is in some places three hundred and fifty or
four hundred feet above water, and at others two
hundred feet (Captain Carroll once, in the month of
June, measured it with the sextant and found it to be
in many places four hundred and eighty-five feet high),
and as there are from eighty to one hundred fathoms
of water immediately in its front, and the ice, of course,
does not float, but is sunken deep into the bottom of
the inlet, it may safely be assumed that there is a front-
age of ice measuring from base to summit between
eight hundred and one thousand feet. It here breaks
off in immense bodies weighing from one to five hundred tons each, and floats with the tide towards the
open sea, disintegrating and melting as it travels.

Owing perhaps to the fact that the water is deeper at the centre than at the sides, the glacier protrudes much farther at this point than in the shallower water near the shores, where there is more resistance, which gives the front an irregular formation, somewhat as of two concaves meeting in the centre. Two interesting theories, if not abundantly demonstrated by proof, are at all events accepted as true by scientists, viz.: *first*, that the front of the glacier is gradually receding from the inlet; and *second*, that the mass of ice itself is just as surely moving towards the inlet, but the recession so far exceeds the accession that there can be little doubt that the ice in some past period extended to the very mouth of the bay itself, and that Willoughby Island owes its present barren surface, and its deep grooves and furrows, to the action of this very glacier.

There are as many different explanations of this recession as there are writings upon the subject, and I should be out of the fashion did I not advance an additional pet one of my own. It is well known that the salubrity of the climate in Puget Sound and on the North Pacific coast generally is due to the warm Japanese current, producing effects similar to those occasioned by the Gulf Stream on the Atlantic. This current becomes charged with the heat of the tropics at the equator, and retains it in its northerly course through the Orient and along the coast of Asia, until it sweeps around and skirts the coast of British Columbia and the State of Washington on its return home, to become again surcharged with the warmth it has distributed in the colder waters of the North. The sphere of this warm stream's action may be widening; widening for the wise purpose of thawing out a wealth of soil and metal which as yet is not needed. It may take centuries, perhaps, to convert the valleys of the mountain ranges, now ice-clogged, into nourishing rivers, but the process may be going on, and if it is, no power to produce it can be more potent than this great gulf stream of the Pacific. It will probably never be ascertained how long a time it has taken for the glacier to fall back from Willoughby Island to its present position, and it certainly has not yet been determined with any degree of accuracy at what rate of speed the vast body of ice is moving towards the point of dissolution; but it is generally agreed, and I presume we will have to accept it, that forty feet a day is the average motion (by average I mean that it moves twice or three times as fast in the centre as at the sides). Now the glacier being over five thousand feet wide, and at least eight hundred feet high, and breaking off at the rate of forty feet each day, it follows that *one hundred and sixty millions of cubic feet of ice break off from the facade of the Muir Glacier every twenty-four hours.* (Hereafter the Swiss *mer de glace* will have to be printed in very small type.) Prof. G. Frederick Wright and a party of scientific friends visited the glacier in August, 1886, for the purpose of making investigations of its glacial phenomena. His paper, published by the Alaskan Society of Natural History and Ethnology, is very interesting, especially upon the subject of the recession of the ice front, from which I conclude that each succeeding year the glory of its immensity somewhat diminishes. After stating his reasons for his faith, he says: "Thus there can be no reasonable doubt that during the earlier part of this century the ice filled the inlet several miles further down than now. And there can scarcely be less doubt that the glacier then filled the inlet 1,000 or 1,500 feet above its present level near the front." And to those for whom figures serve as a guide, I may add upon the authority of Prof. Wright, as follows: "The total amount of water which in some form annually passes into the inlet from the 1,200 square miles of ice which compose the glacier is 267,632,640,000 cubic feet; of this amount 77,088,000,000 feet pass in the form of ice, with 335,473,236 feet of sediment."

MUIR GLACIER AT A DISTANCE.
(*Kodak'd by Author.*)

CHAPTER X.

THE previous chapter has briefly outlined the main facts within my knowledge concerning the Muir Glacier which I had gathered from my reading, and upon which I had to create the image of what I expected to see. True, I had seen photographs of it; yes, and I had seen photographs of the Canyon of the Yellowstone, and of the Nevada Falls, and of Niagara, just as I have seen paste diamonds; I knew their shapes, and that is all I ever gathered from their portraits. Neither the expression nor the complexion, nor the sound of the voice of nature are to be found upon the dull surface of the photograph; you simply get the general lines, some of the shadows, very erroneous perspective, and that is all. We had come to a standstill while we were at lunch. I had observed the slackening of speed; next the stoppage of the machinery; then the absolute stillness of the ship; and finally a darkening of the saloon. We were evidently at a halt under the shadow of some immense elevation. A passenger on tiptoe looked through the port-hole, and uttered an exclamation of amazement; then we all rushed to similar apertures; climbed on the chairs, looked over the men's shoulders, in fact, did all kinds of unreasonable things, and at last stampeded up the companion-way, to the deck. I pray Heaven that neither age nor infirmity may ever efface from my memory the sight and the sensation of that moment. To say that I was transfixed, speechless, fascinated to intoxication by the spell of this marvellous development, is no exaggeration. Those who reached the deck first seemed paralyzed, halted, and thus blocked the way for those who were to follow; others kept within the saloon from choice, as though they dreaded some phenomenal convulsion. I wedged my way as best I could, after the first shock of amazement had subsided, up to the very bow of the ship.

Upon each side of me, half a mile away, rose the same old mountains which I had seen, everywhere from Tacoma north; at my feet, the same Pacific Ocean, but in front of me, apparently so close that I could almost reach it with my fingers, the perpendicular wall of a canyon, not of rock, nor clay, nor grass, nor forest, but of ice—a wall of ice a mile in length;—and when I say a mile I mean over eighteen hundred yards of it; and when I speak of ice, I do not mean the sutty porous stuff that lodges in the valleys of the Alps; I mean the veritable, pure, clear, crystal ice of the ice pitcher. A wall a hundred yards high and in some places towering up an additional fifty; a wall extend-

A BIT OF THE MUIR GLACIER.

ing down deeper in the ocean than it reaches from the
ocean to the sky,—hard as adamant, sharp and edged
like flint, aqua-marine in color, deepening towards
the water into indigo, tipped on the summits and pro-
jections with a froth of snow. If I did not know that
it was ice, I should believe that it was glass. If
I did not know that it was the work of the Creator, I should believe that here had assembled a con-
vocation of architects, who in their collective ingenuity
had reproduced a combination of the *chefs-d'œuvre*
of their art; for here were the buttresses of the English abbeys and flying buttresses of Notre Dame,
turrets of the Normans, towers of the early English,
spires of the cathedral in Cologne, wonderful unoccu-
pied niches, pilasters of the purest white marble and
green malachite, and decorative carving and high polish
worthy of Cellini. It was a cloudy day, yet the front
glistened with prismatic splendor. What will it be, I
asked myself, if in the afternoon the setting sun shall
light it up? But we are too close to it for our own
safety, we learn, and are slowly moved back half a mile,
where our anchor is dropped and preparations are
made to row us on shore to climb to the top of the
glacier. While we are moving, a sharp detonation
rings out like the firing of a rifle, and one of the beautiful spires on the crest of the very centre of the wall
is shivered into atoms, and its fragments fall with a
splash four hundred feet. Later, there is a report as of
a cannon, but without result; this we are told is the
parting of the sea of ice somewhere far back in its

mountain home; presently two similar explosions, evidently right close to us, followed by rumbling echoes, and over topples a huge mass weighing tons, which sinks so far that several seconds elapse before it rises to the surface, swaying to and fro until it finds its equilibrium, and then floats down the current, one more turquoise gem added to the chain which precedes it.

And this continued all day, sometimes at intervals of seconds only, sometimes of half an hour, and when we retired at night the explosion and the splash became as monotonous and periodical as the tinkling of the s'reet-car bell, or the footstep of the passer-by, does at home. There was one tremendous breaking off towards evening; the sun, as we had hoped, was out in full glory, and at the distance from which we now viewed the glacier it was a mountain of snow-covered ice, chopped off in front. For many miles we could see over and beyond the façade, as though looking at a great river of snow; yet the façade itself was a face of corrugated emerald reflecting the sun's rays at every imaginable angle, and changing and scintillating with every movement of the ship. Suddenly, near the centre, the top began to incline forward, and the whole face of probably twenty yards in width, from the top of the glacier to the bottom of the bay, fell outwards as a ladder would fall, without a break anywhere. There was a tremendous upheaving of the water, of course, then the report of the invariable explosion reached us, but no trace remained of the fallen ice, save the swell in the water, which had almost reached and rocked the steamer. I do not know how much time elapsed before the lovely thing rose to the surface, but it seemed an age, and then it came in a dozen pieces, each of the same exquisite diaphanous blue, which as they approached us gradually changed to a clear transparent sapphire. If it will help to serve the purpose of giving a just idea of the colossal proportions of the scene I endeavor to describe, let me say that the Capitol at Washington, the City Hall in Philadelphia, the Cathedral, Equitable, and the Mills Buildings in New York, and all the mammoth newspaper offices in the same city, might be floated in front of the Muir Glacier, and yet its emerald walls would overtop and engulf them all. As a contrast to all that is pure and chaste in the scene before us, there rushes out from the eastern end of the glacier a sub-glacial stream of thick dirty water, much resembling, as it boils up from its cavernous outlet, the mud geyser of the Yellowstone; this is a perpetually flowing river charged with sediment and *débris*, from the scouring process produced by the friction of the moving ice along its bed of rock; it gives the water in the inlet a thick gray color, utterly destroying the charm of its otherwise transparent character.

If you are amiable enough to say that what I have written gives a sufficiently correct idea of what you expect to see, I beg to differ with you. No camera, no pencil, no vocabulary can do more than produce a desire to see for one's self. I can only say that it has been my fortune to behold much that is grand in

nature and in art at home and abroad, but the hours
spent at Muir Glacier made the great event of my life.
If God spares me I hope to see it often.   And fearing
I might be accused of exaggerating, which is far from
my desire, for I am searching in vain for superlatives
which would do the subject justice, let me quote from
others who have preceded me, and all of whom have
established their reputation as authorities :

   MISS KATE FIELD says : " In Switzerland a glacier is
a vast bed of dirty air-holed ice that has fastened
itself, like a cold porous plaster, to the side of an Alp.
Distance alone lends enchantment to the view.   In
Alaska a glacier is a wonderful torrent that seems to
have been suddenly frozen when about to plunge into
the sea. . . .   Think of Niagara Falls frozen still, add
thirty-six feet to its height, and you have a slight idea
of the terminus of Muir Glacier, in front of which
your steamer anchors : picture a background of mountains fifteen thousand feet high, all snow-clad, and then
imagine a gorgeous sun lighting up the ice crystals
with rainbow coloring.   The face of the glacier takes
on the hue of aqua-marine, the hue of every bit of
floating ice, big and little, that surround the steamer
and make navigation serious.   These dazzling serpents
move at the rate of sixty-four feet a day, tumbling
headlong into the sea, and, as they fall, the ear is
startled by submarine thunder, the echoes of which resound far and near.   Down, down, down goes the berg,
and woe to the boat in its way when it rises again to
the surface."

Charles Hallock in "Our New Alaska," pp. 172–3: "The glacier wall overhung us with its mighty majesty, three times the height of the steamer's mast, or more, and we seemed none too far away to escape the constantly cleaving masses which dropped from its face with deafening detonations. The foam which gathered from the impetus of the plunges surged upward fully two-thirds of the height of the cliff, and the resulting swell tossed the large steamer like a toy, and rolled up in breakers of surf upon the beach. . . . The glacier is by no means smooth, but is seamed and riven in every part by clefts and fissures. It is hollowed into caverns and grottoes, hung with massive stalactites, and fashioned into pinnacles and domes. Every section and configuration has its heart of translucent blue or green, interlaced or bordered by fretted frost-work of intensest white; so that the appearance is at all times gnome-like and supernatural. . . . I cannot conceive how any one can sit by and contemplate without emotion the stupendous throes which give birth to the icebergs, attended with detonations like explosions of artillery, and reverberations of thunder across the sky, and the mighty wreckage which follows each convulsion. Nevertheless I have seen a lady loll with complaisance in her steamer chair, comfortably wrapped for the chilly air, and observe the astounding scene with the same languid contemplation that she would discuss her social fixtures and appointments. Zounds! I believe that such a human negation would calmly view the wreck of worlds, and hear the crack of doom

at the final rendering, if it did not affect "her set."
She could watch at a suitable distance the agony of
Christian martyrs, the carnage of great battles, the
sweep of cyclones, the diluvial submergence. Dyna-
mite would not appall her, but to me it would be the
acme of satisfaction, ineffably supreme, to startle such
clods of inanition by a cry of mouse, and electrify
them into a momentary emotion. No vinaigrette would
ever mitigate the shock."

MARTIN M. BALLOU in "The New Eldorado—a Summer Journey to Alaska," pp. 276–7: "The roar of
artillery upon a battle-field could hardly be more
deafening or incessant than were the thrilling reports
caused by the falling of vast masses of ice from the
glacier's front. Nothing could be grander or more impressive than this steady bombardment from the ice
mountain in its resistless progress towards the sea.
Neither Norway nor Switzerland have any glacial or
Arctic scenery that can approach this bay in its frigid
splendor. . . . The author, in a varied experience of
many parts of the world, recalls but two other occasions which affected him so powerfully as this first
visit to Glacier Bay in Alaska, namely, witnessing the
sun rise over the vast Himalayan range, the roof-tree
of the globe, at Dargelling, in Northern India, and the
view of the midnight sun from the North Cape in
Norway, as it hung over the Polar Sea. Our power of
appreciation is limitless, though that of description
is circumscribed. Here both are challenged to their
utmost capacity. Words are insufficient, pen and pen-

cil inadequate to convey the grandeur and fascination of the scene."

Mrs. E. R. Scidmore in "Journeys in Alaska": "Avalanches of crumbling ice and great pieces of the front were continually falling with the roar and crash of artillery, revealing new caverns and rifts of deeper blue light, while the spray dashed high and the great waves rolled along the icy wall, and widening in their sweep, washed the blocks of floating ice up on the beaches on either side. . . . The nearer one approached, the higher the ice walls seemed, and all along the front there were pinnacles and spires weighing several tons, that seemed on the point of toppling every moment. The great buttresses of ice that rose first from the water and touched the moraine, were as solidly white as marble, veined and streaked with rocks and mud, but further on, as the pressure was greater, the color slowly deepened to turquoise and sapphire blues."

Alexander Badlam in his "Wonders of Alaska," p. 42, quotes Prof. Muir himself as saying, that the front and brow of the glacier were "dashed and sculptured into a maze of yawning chasms, ravines, canyons, crevasses and a bewildering chaos of architectural forms, beautiful beyond the measure of description, and so bewildering in their beauty as to almost make the spectator believe he was revelling in a dream." "There were," he said, "great clusters of glistening spires, gables, obelisks, monoliths and castles, standing out boldly against the sky, with bastion and mural, surmounted by fretted cornice, and every interstice and chasm reflecting a sheen of scintillating light and deep blue shadow, making a combination of color, dazzling, startling, and enchanting."

The next sensation in store for the tourist is the climb to the top of the glacier. All the row-boats were lowered, and about a dozen passengers in each, armed with alpenstocks, were ferried in successive groups from the ship to the eastern beach, a distance of perhaps half a mile, instructions being given to each steersman to keep a sharp look-out for falling icebergs. And here your trouble commences unless you are well advised. The ascent is exceedingly difficult; what looks like a mountain of rock over which you must

wend your way to the ice-fields, is really a mountain of ice covered by a layer of slimy mud, crusted with pieces of flinty granite, standing up on end like broken bottle glass on the top of a wall. I wore india-rubber high boots when I started, and I needed crutches before I finished. It may be chilly as you leave

THE CLIMB.
(Kodak'd by
Miss M. Watson.

and
.eep
ing,

the
.ere
ned
ups
per-
ach
rgs.
vell
hat
ust

THE CLIMB.
(Kodak'd by
Miss M. Watson)

the ship, according as the sun may be out or in; if chilly,
get your escort to carry an extra shawl for you to wrap
yourself in when you row back to the ship; if the
weather is bright and warm, clothe yourself lightly, for
it grows warmer with the glare from the ice and the
physical exertion. Be very careful where you step, and
if you are wise, follow in the footsteps of others;
do not undertake to lead, else one foot may be trying
to ascertain the depth of a quagmire and the other
exploring a fissure. After an ascent of perhaps two and
a half miles, which seem more like ten, you will find
yourself on the edge of a frozen sea, frozen, as it were,
while in the throes of a tempest, a bay of storm-tossed
waves solidified as by a signal; and this extends as far
as the eye can reach up into the mountains towards the
north, and several miles across to the hills upon the
opposite shore. The ice is by no means clear or brilliant,
on the contrary its color is milky and its formation
honey-combed, plastic, porous, and yielding to the tread;
besides which it is besmeared with sediment from
mountain thaws which have traversed its rifts, and
disfigured by fallen logs and drift-wood. I confess
that if I visited Muir Glacier a hundred times I should
always remain on deck and watch the pyrotechnics of
the façade rather than undergo the thankless fatigue
of climbing to the top, which is infinitely more labori-
ous than the ascent of Vesuvius on foot through the
lava, or any work to be done on the trails of the
Yosemite. To those who are willing to undertake it,
however, I suggest that when they have ascended the

THE TOP OF MUIR GLACIER.

ON TOP.—*(Kodaked by Miss Margaret Watson.)*

first mile, which will about bring them on a line with the top of the wall of the glacier, they should look back at their little tiny ship, floating like the *Maid of the Mist* beneath Niagara, to fully realize the immense proportions of the glacier.

It is said that persons have been missed and never again found who made this ascent, and I know that at least one case is authentic, that of a young clergyman, who, straying away from his companions, was never again seen, though the most diligent search was made for him by his friends and the ship's crew. A slip into one of those crevasses, which is covered by a thin coat of ice, means to be precipitated in an instant to a depth where no human aid can reach you. In fact I would advise all who wish to preserve the impression of Muir Glacier in its pure, idealized, unsullied grandeur, to stay aboard and gaze on its beautiful face. It is a Persian custom, after plucking the fruit, to tear it asunder in the middle, hand

the sunny side to the friend and throw the other
half away, the best portion being the only part good
enough for those they love.   It is my duty to present
to you the better half of the glacier and to cast away
the other.   Tired, footsore, and muddy, we were all
early in bed, and while dozing to sleep I was much
impressed with the awful stillness of the hour; everybody had retired, not even the tread of the man on
watch was heard, the very machinery was sleeping, but
every now and then there was a splash and a report
and an echo that brought with them the proof that the
forces of nature were ever awake, and that what was,
"is, and ever shall be, world without end."

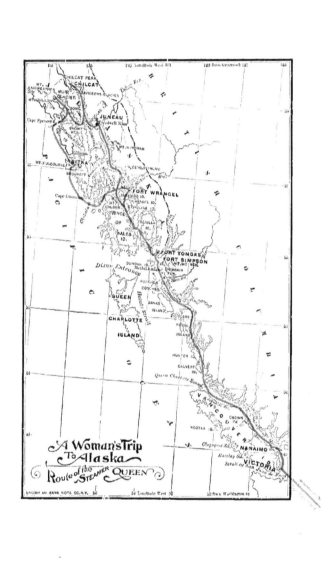

A Woman's Trip
To Alaska
Route of the STEAMER QUEEN

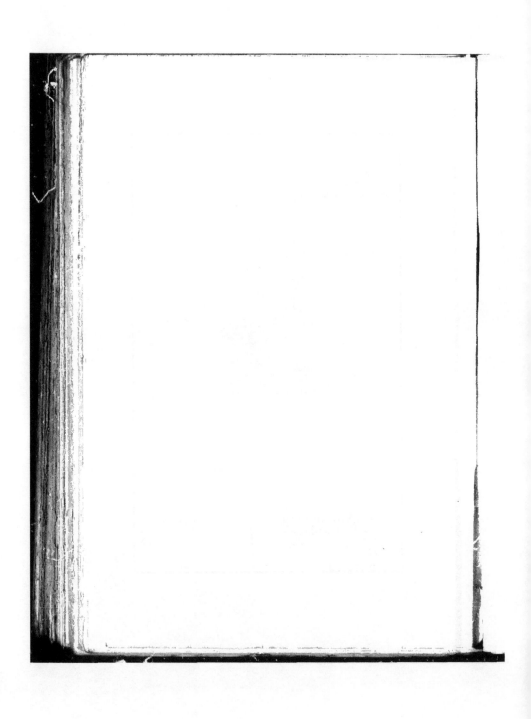

CHAPTER XI.

HERE was no hurry to be up and off on Sunday morning, June 8th. When I awoke we were still lying at anchor in front of the glacier, and I was told by my fellow-passengers that an immense slice of the wall had yielded to the pressure and jumped overboard during the night. And when I came on deck I saw this must be so, for a bright, new green surface to the ice front was presented, entirely free from the snowdrifts which I had seen there yesterday, and there were many more floating bergs than when I had retired. We now dropped down the bay a mile or two into the field of ice again, and for two or three hours occupied our time in filling the hold of the ship with beautiful sparkling blocks of it, about forty tons, which was

(*From Kodak by Miss M. D. Beach.*)

to last the ship for all purposes until she returned again
in two weeks. A couple of boats were lowered and
manned with sailors armed with picks, hooks, and
axes; these men first shaped the ice while in the water
and chopped away the crusts of snow, the blocks being
then hauled on board and lowered into the hold.

It was near noon when we began to turn our backs
on this lake of the gods and steamed along the shores
of Seidmore Island. A more perfect day never shone
from the heavens; there was not a speck of cloud anywhere; poets and painters, educated in the fogs of
London, who write about and paint the sunny skies of
Italy, never saw such an atmosphere as this; the air
was warm and balmy, the breeze invigorating, and the
bosom of the deep blue sea here and there bejewelled
with the emeralds, opals, pearls, and turquoises that had
fallen from the great towers of ice which now received
our sad farewells and our hopeful promise to return.
On our right, loom up the wonderful Fairweather
range of White Mountains, which Captain Carroll had
held in reserve for us until this auspicious moment.
The farthest peak is Mt. Fairweather, boasting an
altitude equal to Mt. Blanc, of over 15,000 feet; a little
closer to us is Mt. Crillon, reaching towards heaven
almost 16,000 feet; and nearer still, Mt. LaPerouse,
11,300 feet,—all connected by a long chain of lesser
ones, forming an immense range perpetually covered
with snow of the purest white. On our left is Seidmore
Island clad in midsummer verdure fragrant with strawberries and wild flowers, and musical with feathery

song; in front, the ever placid ocean, whose marvellous transparency attests its depth; and the whole amphitheatre bounded by a circle of majestic hills clad in their royal purple. I wish I could remember the beautiful words with which the Rev. Dr. Tiffany likened it to the glorious portal of a future life. I do remember that a gentleman standing near me remarked "I did not believe God ever made any thing so beautiful as this," to which I involuntarily replied, but I am sure not irreverently, "I did not believe that He *could.*"

I shall never again experience such a day as that! The same sight under the same favorable conditions would hardly again impress me as did the startling novelty of this first view of it. And to think that it has existed for thousands of years, and the present decade has been the first to see it. Picture to yourself all that you can recollect of the Hudson, the Danube, and the Rhine; carry your mind away up into the fiords and rocky coast of Norway; put the little Swiss *mer de glace* under a microscope; think of the Matterhorn, the Jungfrau, Mt. Blanc and the entire Bernese Alps; make one lake of Maggiore and all her sisters; and still this Lake of the Gods, as I would have it named, out-pictures it all a hundred-fold. The day, the scene, and the mood were all in harmony for recognition of the Divine beneficence which had given us life and health to behold His glorious works, and, accordingly, Dr. Tiffany was requested to hold Divine service, which he cheerfully consented to do at three o'clock; but just as the hour was arriving we sighted a steamer ahead, which proved to be our old friend the *Pinta*, which we had left at Fort Wrangell, and as we had on board news from the lonely wives and children at Sitka, both ships slackened speed, boats were lowered, and the glad tidings of good health at home were borne to the anxious mariners. To accomplish this Dr. Tiffany postponed the service until a later hour, and

THE TREADWELL GOLD MINES.

when we at last assembled, I am sure a pure spirit of sincere thanksgiving pervaded the entire congregation.

It was in the night-time that we rounded Dome Peak, entered the Lynn Canal and headed for Douglas Island, which we reached on Monday morning, June 9th, just one week from Tacoma. We would have passed right on to Juneau, which is in sight a little farther to the north, but there is something very interesting which we must go ashore to see, so we are tied up to a long wharf, the gang-plank is thrown out, and the same old procession moves out; this time to visit the Alaska Company's gold mine (commonly called the Treadwell Mine). John Treadwell, a San Francisco builder, bought this property in 1881 from a prospector, of whom a fair estimate may be formed by the fact that he was known only as "French Pete." The price was $400, and for some time subsequently it was operated as a placer mine the character of ore visible being, I am told, what is scientifically

A WHOLE QUARRY OF GOLD.

known as decomposed quartz. Treadwell sold part of his interest to others at a large advance; and to-day this quarry of gold produces an income of half a million of dollars every year. From our fellow-passenger, Mr. Bernhardt, I gathered the information (for I don't know a thing about mining) that it is what is called a low-grade ore, and owing to the immense water-power in the vicinity, the proximity of the ocean, and the fact that there is no expense of

shafting and tunnelling, it costs less than two dollars
per ton to produce the bullion from the rock, and that
six hundred tons are worked each day, of the value of
from four to six dollars per ton. We went all through
the works, visited the quarry, hunted around for nuggets but did not find any, and were taken into the mill,
where two hundred and forty stamps, as they are
called, are hammering like so many sledge-hammers,
making such a noise that you literally cannot hear
yourself speak, and creating such a vibration that you
dance around like those bits of cork with horse-hair
legs which children play with on the drum of a piano.
One gentleman exclaimed as he emerged : " That is the
first place I have ever been where my wife can talk to
me without making me hear." (Of course he did not
refer to me ; if he had I would have made myself *felt*.)
Having seen every thing of interest at the mine, excepting the gold ingots, they having all been shipped
away in a previous steamer, we moved on to Juneau, a
couple of miles distant, passing the " Bear's Nest " and
one or two other gold mines which are as yet in embryo.

Juneau, like Sitka, is nestled at the foot of a range of
sheltering mountains. As I approached it, I wondered
what would become of the adults if the small boys
should take it into their heads to bombard them with
snowballs from the tops of the mountains, which
abruptly rise two thousand feet from the end of every
street. I consider Juneau as prettily located as any
city I have ever seen, and when the rich fields of gold
which surround it are developed, it will very likely

attain much commercial prominence. From all I could
gather I have little doubt that the history of California
will be repeated in this vicinity; the place is full of
speculators and prospectors, many of the latter having
good " claims " for sale, but at very high prices. The
owners seem to have unlimited confidence in their
" finds," and are certain that they will get their price
by the exercise of patience; but in the meantime they
lead an improvident, from hand to mouth, idle kind of
a life; yet I am told that if they were content to part
with their ownership to capitalists who would agree to
expend money for development, and reserve a share of
profit for the pre-emptor, it is believed this system
would be better for the present owners and much to
the advantage of the locality. From the bay, Juneau
has the appearance of some systematic regularity of
construction, but when you land it has quite the contrary; in fact, to quote the language of my companion,
it " looked as though it had been built late on a Saturday night and never finished." It is an accidental
town; unlike Tacoma, Seattle, Victoria, and other
thriving cities of Puget Sound, which have been
located and laid out after careful consideration of the
whole subject, Juneau, like Helena in Montana,
" growed up," as Topsy did. It is really a mining
camp, founded by Joseph Juneau and Richard Harris
just ten years ago this autumn, and yet it is to-day
the most important commercial point upon the entire
coast. This is owing to the existence of the gold placer
mines of the Silver Bow Basin immediately back of the

shore, many of them having been worked out, but leaving behind them the best evidences of the precious mineral awaiting the advent of capital. A serious embarrassment, however, exists as to the real ownership of the different properties, and these titles, I presume, will have to be adjusted before the risk is assumed of advancing the large sums necessary for intelligent exploration and experiment. The streets of the town seem to follow the gulches or ravines, and the architecture is exceedingly primitive. There are three or four interesting shops at which may be purchased every known Esquimaux curio, and two or three where may be seen an excellent collection of sable, marten, lynx, silver-fox, and other furs. The signs indicate that the traders are not wedded to specialties, but keep a stock of varieties always on hand. One of them, of which I took a note, read as follows: " Whipsaws, potatoes, new onions, carrots, and wall-tents."

I spent a considerable portion of my time in the store of Messrs. Kohler & James, who, I believe, are the successors of the Northwest Trading Company. Here I had an opportunity of witnessing the system of barter and trade carried on between the Indian hunter and the white trader. Upon arriving in town with the skins the red man visits every shop and trader before he parts with his supply, and he who is finally the highest bidder gets it; when the bargain is consummated the Indian receives in payment a number of blue or red tickets, which are taken by the store-keeper in exchange for such commodities as he

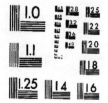

IMAGE EVALUATION
TEST TARGET (MT-3)

may require to carry back to his Innuit home, perhaps somewhere near the head-waters of the Yukon.
From this store I carried off some beautiful furs at most
reasonable rates, and hoped to be the possessor of a
much-coveted sable rug of thirty skins, but failed to con-
vince the trader that my valuation of it was a just one.
In fact, the only regret I carried with me from Alaska

ALASKA CURIOS.
(*Kodak'd by Author.*)

was that I had not given what was
asked for this rug, but my information then was to the effect that prices
were specially prepared for tourists,
which, I am now convinced, is not
the case, certainly not at the store of
which I speak.   Just as the ship was
leaving Juneau I determined to
hurry back and purchase it, but I
was admonished by the Captain that
"time and tide wait for no man,"
nor woman either, so I simply just
gazed at that shop with a melan-
choly and rueful countenance, and
the increasing distance, I assure you,
lent the view no enchantment.   (I
ought to say here in a parenthetical
whisper that the day I returned home to New York I
was surprised to find that dear coveted robe spread out
upon the sofa in my library.)   Before leaving Tacoma
we had been handed a printed programme of a "native
dance, by the renowned dancers of the Thlinkit tribe of
Alaska Indians, under the management of D. Martini,

the Barnum of Alaska, and the celebrated Takou Chief, *Yash Noosh,* head chief of one of the most warlike tribes of Alaska, but have succumbed (sic) to the influences of civilization. Admission $1. Children 50 cts. The performance will commence immediately after the arrival of the excursion steamer at Juneau, Alaska." When we arrived, this Alaska Barnum, wearing a high stove-pipe hat, in company with Yash Noosh himself, not in the garb of a warlike Indian chief, but in that of a quiet guardian of the public peace, commonly called a policeman, met us at the dock and begged to inform us that the performance had been postponed until two o'clock, and they did this with an air of people who seemed to think we had come there simply to see their "greatest show on earth." While this ceremony was taking place a savage noise of human voices and beating of drums came from a long tent on the beach, which, of course, we recognized as the place of performance. Very few of the passengers were willing to be humbugged by the man with the high hat and the policeman, yet our little party, which, by friendships created on the tour, might now number eight or ten persons, resolved to "take it in," as one of the gentlemen expressed it. We went; we were not "taken in"; those who failed to go were the only ones who were cheated, and they cheated themselves. It was a remarkable performance — picturesque, barbarous, unexplainable, and unique. The theatre itself was a long tent, with a platform curtained off by the commonest white muslin, rows of pine benches for

seats, and a little dressing-room in the rear. The
audience consisted of twenty-one persons who paid one
dollar each, while the performers numbered about
thirty men, women, and children in every imaginable
garb, from the ultra-aboriginal to that of the present
time. The tent was insufferably warm and *smellful*,
the glare of sunlight through the thin canvas intense,
so that the use of parasol and lavender salts was
indispensable; the stray Indian squaws and their offspring sitting around the floors were repulsive; nevertheless, with all its unattractive surroundings, I would
not have missed it. There was no humbug about the
dramatis personæ, the wardrobe, or the implements,
and, therefore, I presume, none about the authenticity
of the dances themselves. Two or three of the men,
clad from neck to feet in skin-fitting white kid (much
soiled), were most graceful specimens of perfect
anatomy and agility; one or two of the women were
quite attractive, but others were hideously painted,
horribly shaped, and were either semi-idiotic or under
the influence of *hoochinoo* (though I saw no evidence
that any of them could procure liquor in the town).
Men there were with the torso of a giant and the lower
limbs of a dwarf, giving them a miserably awkward
gait. The women all resembled the lowest caste of
Chinese, but with coarser and broader faces and larger
features; some of them with faces painted entirely
black as a complexion preserver, others colored only
across the upper portion of the face, indicating widow-
hood, and all looking the saddest specimens of indif-

ferent wretchedness, so benighted as not to realize the
degradation, misery, and filth of their existence. I was
specially moved to pity by a little girl about nine years
old, evidently a half-breed, a truly pretty child, with
beautiful eyes and fine features, a little gypsy creature,
who sat in a filthy calico dress, her only garment, and
a bright red handkerchief across her black matted
hair; the industry of her little fingers told the story
of the lack of care of which this neglected bit of
humanity was the victim; and in all her squalid lone-
liness my mother instincts went out to her, and I
wished with all my heart that I could have saved her,
body and soul. The printed "Programme" of the
dances announced the following:

" *Tash-Neesh*—An ancient dance participated in by the Indians more than two
hundred years ago.
Ya-Koo-ky—An ancient dance in honor of visiting chieftains from afar.
Ya-Heen-nah-kla-ky—A wild and weird dance of the interior tribes—very
ancient.
On-ti-kye-ot—A representation of the Shaman, or Indian doctor's dance
when expelling an evil spirit from a patient.
Kow-z-ki-ki-klanik—A dance making friends among the tribes—never per-
formed since the days of Baranoff.
Salmon dance—This dance takes place on the occasion of the spring run of
salmon.
Love dance—Chaste and pure, with its beautiful and soul-inspiring music.
Chichigoff waltz—By Hoonyiah Indians."

I was so thoroughly unprepared for the scenes which
the lifting of the curtain developed, and paid so little
attention to the explanations made by the Indian policeman, who was master of the ceremonies, or his
interpreter, that I am unable to individualize the dif-

ferent dances. They all seemed alike, excepting that
one representing the incantations of the Shaman. As
the cotton sheet was drawn aside by a pair of dusky
hands, Indians of both sexes were discovered seated
around the stage beating drums and singing a most
discordant, monotonous, and dirge-like song; then
from the little annex came a procession of dancers,
male and female, dressed in buckskin and feathers,
with horribly painted faces, each wearing on the head
a hollow crown filled to the top with the down of the
eagle's breast. The dance commenced by a very slow
forward movement of the body, the progress made
being not more than an inch at each step, and while
the whole anatomy was kept in constant motion the
principal feature of it was a jerky,
forward movement of the head, a
throwing out and draw-
ing back of the chin,
as it were, and a cor-
responding lifting
of the shoulders:
this, of course, agi-
tated the eagle's
down in the crowns,
and in a few minutes
the entire tent, stage,
and auditorium was
a snow-storm. As
the dancers became
warmed to their

*From Kodak by
Miss M. D. Beach.)*

work, which was manifested by the feathers completely covering their perspiring faces, giving them a Santa Claus expression that was very funny, their legs began to loosen, and tripped a cadence not unlike the old-fashioned Virginia break-down, while the totem-sticks, paddles, salmon-hooks, knives, and implements of warfare were flourished aloft in a most careless and hazardous fashion. The peculiarity of the exhibition was that the dancing was palpably intended to give expression to some thought, and the looks of disdain, contempt, hate, rage, and tender love would have been appreciated even by Salvini. Some danced barefooted, others wore red socks; one or two women were robed in exquisite Thlinket embroidered blankets, robes of fur graced (?) the shoulders of others, and one wore an entire skirt of ermine. The Shaman dance would not have been given but that we insisted upon the programme being carried out. It appeared that the Doctor was disgruntled about something—perhaps the "beggarly array of empty benches" disappointed him, and no wonder, for when he did finally play his part, it was so exhausting that he could hardly arise from the sitting posture which he assumed from the first. His was a dance of the arms, hands, shoulders, mouth, and eyes. It was a sorcerer's appeal, keeping time to the thumping of drums on the rear seats—the whites of his eyes were rolled upwards during the whole time, his head rocked from side to side, his fingers clawed the air, and his teeth fastened themselves in his lips during the fervor of his invocations. It was a weird spectacle, and if it

did n't succeed in driving the worst evil spirit that
ever lurked around a sick-chamber out of the window
it 's a very great wonder. We did not hesitate to ex-
press to the Alaska Barnum our commendation of his
exhibition, and all voluntarily recorded our opinions of
it in a book which, at our suggestion, he procured for
our signatures, so that it might impress the tourists
who followed us, Mr. Policeman Yash Noosh having
informed the spectators that it was to be a permanent
institution, and I hope it may prove so. It was my
good fortune to be able to purchase the totem-pole
which conspicuously figured in the evolutions, but I
suppose it has since been replaced by another.

CHAPTER XII.

THE prevalence of ice in such large quantities in Glacier Bay made it prudent that we should not risk the entrance of Taku Inlet. As Captain Carroll expressed it, " the people up here must have had a hard winter." Besides which, this being the *Queen's* first trip in these waters, it was not an appropriate time to experiment as to whether she could navigate the narrower channels. In fact, it was predicted before we left Tacoma that she was too big for the service, an opinion which she has since very successfully disproved. At the head of Taku Inlet, after a sail of fifteen miles, there are to be seen three very superb glaciers, none of them, of course, equal to the Muir Glacier, yet, as it sometimes happens that owing to fogs and ice the Muir Glacier is inaccessible and may not be seen at all, the tourist will be well repaid by a visit to Taku, though, from what I learned of it, I again renew my advice to remain on the ship rather than wander over the muddy moraines. Leaving Juneau, we ran due no. 'i along the Lynn Canal to

Chilcat, which is the most northerly point of the excursion route, being above the 59° of latitude. The scene along the entire route is in keeping with that which has framed our journey since we left Victoria. Passing the Auk and Eagle glaciers on our right, we pause for a while in front of the Davidson Glacier, which meets the eye on the left like a mighty river rushing through the mountain gorges to the sea, and madly emptying itself into the ocean at the foot of a dense forest. This body of ice is as graceful in form as the Muir is heroic in colossal stature. It is nearly three miles wide at its mouth and slopes downwards from an altitude of twelve hundred feet, opening out towards the spectator like the spreading of a fan. Pyramid Harbor, *en route*, is an exquisite bit of mountain scenery, not unlike the Hudson near West Point, though few of the peaks are less than three thousand feet high. It is nearly dark when we turn around, and, having to retrace our steps over the same course for several miles, we unanimously agree to pay to Sleep our debt for the many hours borrowed from her in the past three nights. Keeping to the eastern channel around Admiralty Island we, of course, did not stop at Killisnoo, much to our regret, but the Captain promised in compensation to give us a surprise in a day or two if the conditions favored it.

Killisnoo is an interesting station from the fact that here is a large manufactory of the Northwest Trading Company for producing fish-oil and drying codfish, the latter said to far excel the same article caught and preserved by the Newfoundland fishermen. The natives

DAVIDSON GLACIER.

of this place a few years ago threatened to massacre
the whites in revenge for the accidental killing of a
Shaman by the premature explosion of a torpedo, and
would have done so but for the timely arrival of a
revenue cutter, which threw a few noisy shells into the
village and naturally produced intense quiet. Our return trip was so arranged as to pass in the daytime
many exquisite marvels of scenery, which we had lost
in the night coming up, among them the Wrangell

KILLISNOO.

Narrows and Clarence Straits, whose unfathomable,
still waters mirrored the rocks, which buttressed the
innumerable fiords upon each side of us into all kinds
of shapes, shades, and angles, presenting a kaleidoscopic
land- and water-scape the whole livelong day, all of
which, as I think back, comes to me like the fantasy
of a delightful dream.   In one deep canyon, where you
could almost shake hands with a friend on shore, there
soared aloft a veritable American eagle, floating from
side to side and encircling us with the sweep of his graceful motion for many miles until we reached the open

bay, and then, as though content that we had escaped the hazards of our narrow course, alighted on the highest twig of the foremost tree of a little island at our side, and with flapping wings seemed to bid us God-speed. If I had been Captain Carroll I would have dipped the colors to that loyal bird.

One morning we were very much surprised by the appearance on the surface of the water of sheets of some salmon-colored substance, for which it was not possible to account. At first we supposed it to be sawdust floating out from the mouth of some river; then again it might be salmon-spawn, yet the well proportioned egg was not there. The sailors told us it was whale food, but that was all they knew of it. We gathered some of it in a pail, and were no wiser; but we brought some home in a bottle. When uncorked it had "an ancient and a fishlike smell," and when examined by the microscope it bore all the evidence of being the spawn of a small fish. There is a little fish in these waters called the oulikon (or candle-fish), which is all oil. Its head being thrust by the natives into a split stick and a light applied to its tail, it burns for a considerable time, the vertebræ, I suppose, answering for a wick. This is the Indian's household illuminator. It is not unlikely that this is the fish which deposits its spawn on the surface of the deep sea under the rays of a powerful sun, but what we saw was certainly not allowed to hatch out, for in a few hours, while exchanging courtesies, *en route*, with the *City of Topeka* northward bound, we saw large schools of

THE MOUNT ST. ELIAS RANGE.

whales going straight for this food with wonderful instinct.

A great effort was made to induce Captain Carroll to run up into Bute Inlet, but at this he drew the line; he had never explored it excepting in a small boat, and was ignorant of the soundings, although he believed it had, like all the other fiords on the coast, an abundance of deep water. The Captain spoke of it with much enthusiasm, describing the canyons as resembling those of the Yellowstone, and mounting in a precipitous perpendicular eight thousand feet. In fact, every year develops some new feature of this glorious trip, producing a fever to return to it, which has possessed me ever since I stepped ashore at Tacoma, after twelve of the most restful and enjoyable days of my life.

The wonderful discoveries of Professors Israel C. Russell and Mark B. Kerr during the past summer in their explorations of the Mount St. Elias range, lead me to hope that upon my next trip our ship will visit Yakutat Bay, where the Lucia and Baird glaciers reach the navigable waters of the North Pacific Ocean. I cannot bring myself to believe that I have yet to see a mass of ice equalling the gigantic proportions of the Muir, and yet Mr. Kerr tells us the "Lucia" is ten miles in width, and Mr. Russell says the "Piedmont" is the largest glacier in the Northern Hemisphere.

Fort Simpson, however, was the treat the Captain had in store for us, and a real treat it was. We had left Fort Tongas behind us, and were scraping the edges of the beautiful Dundas Island. We knew that Metlahkatlah, the refugee home of the band of pilgrim Indians who had fled from the debasing influences of their kin at Fort Simpson, was right ahead of us, and we felt sure that we would be dropped down among these Indians, living up to a nineteenth century civilization, with churches, school-houses, lighted streets, a city government, and so on;—but nothing of the kind; we steered direct for Fort Simpson itself, where we arrived just before sunset. Oh, what a pity we had not been there a few hours earlier; what a splendid field for our camera, for it is the home of the totem-pole and of every type of Indian life and custom, civilized and savage. Fort Simpson is in British Columbia, and floats the British flag. As early as 1821, the Hudson Bay Company, which was the incorporated successor to the grant of Charles II. to his cousin Prince Rupert, giving him exclusive right of exploration and settlement on the North American continent, established the post of Fort Simpson, giving it the name of its president. There are two bastions and a stockade here, but whether built then or more recently to resist the incursions of hostile Indians, I was unable to ascertain. I visited, nevertheless, the company's store, which seems to be about the only place of trade in the village; was quite courteously received by the gentleman in charge, who showed me the candle-fish and other indigenous curiosities, and then I joined the column (we are beginning to look awfully like Cook's tourists wandering around the Alps), note-book in hand.

The location of Fort Simpson is very much like that of Sitka and Juneau; the same kind of harbor and the same gaunt, weird and sheltering mountains, but the population is almost entirely native, consisting of fifteen white people and nine hundred and fifty Indians; most of the men were off fishing and canning at the canneries along the shore, taking their entire families with them and closing up their houses. Those who were still at home seemed to be superior to any we had yet seen, their houses having neat outsides, though the interiors afford much room for improvement. It boasts of a Methodist church, an exceedingly plain structure of four walls with a cheap lot of benches, and a simple decoration of "God is love" behind the pulpit, a great contrast to the Greek church of Sitka. During the past winter there had been forty-five deaths from la grippe, and many houses bore the Indian insignia of mourning—a piece of black crêpe, pinked at the edges and placed on a sheet of white paper. These badges were nailed on the homes of recent death, and in many cases a well-sculptured marble tombstone stood before the house, inscribed (as with us) with the name and age of the deceased, which is kept here only during the months of mourning, and is then carried to the grave. The graveyard is very interesting and worth a visit; but the totem-poles are by far the most remarkable feature of the place; they are of large size and grotesque sculpturing, and contain the cremated ashes of the departed. It would not have been a sin against the Decalogue to have fallen down and worshipped them, for they were unlike any thing "that is in heaven above, or that is in the earth beneath, or that is in the waters under the earth." The children told us that the animals represented existed in the olden time, but were now all buried in the sea. Here we saw abundant specimens of "muck a muck," which we took to be cuttings of peat for fuel, until informed, to our great disgust, that it was the Indians' staple food; black in color, and made up into cakes about twelve inches square and an inch thick, it lay all around the place, drying in the sun, and overrun by the dogs and cats of the village; it is made of seaweed, and when well dried is converted into soup. I brought a specimen home with me, but only to look at.

The people who are still in the village have been, within the last thirty years, reclaimed from a life of barbarism marked by atrocities the recitals of which are blood-curdling. When the first missionary, Mr. William Duncan arrived from Scotland, he found them absolutely under the influence of the Shaman. The Shamans were of two classes, man-eaters and dog-eaters. At their will life was sacrificed to remedy the most trifling evils, the lowly serfs being put to death to avert some imagined catastrophe about to happen to a chief. Women were dragged by ropes to the beach, brutally murdered, and thus sent into the other world to be ready in waiting as slaves to receive the sick daughter of the chief who lay upon her dying bed; and when murdered, their bodies were eaten by the Shamans in the presence of the assembled populace. "These are some of the things and scenes," says Mr. Duncan, "which occur in the day during the winter months, while the nights are taken up with amusements, singing, and dancing. Occasionally the medicine-parties invite people to their houses and play tricks before them of various kinds. . . . The great feature of their proceedings is to pretend to murder and then restore to life. The cannibal, on such occasions, is generally supplied with two, three, or four human bodies, which he tears to pieces before his audience. Several persons, either from bravado or for a charm, present their arms for him to bite. I have seen several whom he had thus bitten, and I hear two have died from the effects." All this, however, has now changed, the people seem to be well clad, well fed, and contented, and the children give signs of intelligence and education. Of course, the plague spots are not all eradicated yet: old habits still cling to the aged, and they are really in a deplorable condition. Being told that an old chieftain

an.
og-
:he
ith
to
ch,
rld
ick
ed;
he
ce.
Mr.
ter
se-
ne-
ks
of
en
on-
es,
ral
nt
om
he
go-
nd
on.
et:
in
in

was dying in one of the huts, we entered; not from
curiosity merely, but in the hope that we might perhaps render him service. Alas, it was too late. He
lay on a blanket on the floor, surrounded by half a
dozen women of all ages stretched upon the ground
like as many seals, and life was ebbing peacefully
away. We spoke to the women, who simply glared at
us with a dazed expression, but made no reply. At
the door, as we were going away, we met an old squaw,
probably the chieftain's wife, laboring up the steep
hill, staff in hand, and a load of blankets on her back
(blankets are the currency of her people): she must
have been ninety years of age, and when she reached
the house of mourning it was with difficulty
she sat down, but she kept up a continual
muttering of despairing
tones which were heart-
rending. There was no
doubt about her sorrow.
The fountain of her tears
had dried up, and she
reminded me of Dante's
description of that agony
which knows no vent and
finds no relief, "*Io non pian-
gea, sì dentro impietrai.*"

CHAPTER XIII.

WHEN we returned to the ship it was ten o'clock, not by the light of the moon, but in another of those glorious sunsets which nearly always closed our days. Some of our party said it was the most gorgeous sunset they had ever seen, but, to tell the truth, I was so satiated with the grand and beautiful that all my powers of comparison had departed. I remember, though, that the entire ocean and the heavens, too, were lit up with red and golden shimmering lights. A few miles from Fort Simpson is the settlement of Metlahkatlah, where dwell the pilgrim Indians who fled under the guidance of their Moses, William Duncan, from the atrocities and barbaric life of the former place in 1862 and founded a town which is a model of civilization and good government. Their constitution is a written one, and exceedingly brief. It is a disavowal of vices and an avowal of virtues, and reads as follows:

"1st. To give up their 'Ahlied' or Indian deviltry. 2d. To cease calling in conjurors when sick. 3d. To cease gambling. 4th. To cease giving away property for display. 5th. To cease painting their faces. 6th. To cease drinking intoxicating drink. 7th. To rest on the Sabbath. 8th. To attend religious instruction. 9th. To send their children to school. 10th. To be cleanly. 11th. To be industrious. 12th. To be peaceful. 13th. To be liberal and honest in trade. 14th. To build neat houses. 15th. To pay the village tax."

The population of Metlahkatlah may be two or three thousand—I was unable to ascertain the exact figures,—and the principal industry of the place is a salmon cannery, which is a joint-stock company, the stock of which is held by the natives and pays handsome dividends. The young men are taught useful trades and apprenticed to those who have become proficient. All the churches, school-houses, and dwellings are built by the inhabitants, and the women have learned to weave and to spin. The sanctity of the marriage vow is strictly observed, polygamy is unknown, and children are well cared for physically, mentally, and morally. It is entirely the product of the English Church Missionary Society, and their fearless representative, Mr. William Duncan. Most of this good work has been accomplished in the last quarter of a century; and the field is still large for similar undertakings.

To describe the exquisite and awe-inspiring scenery of the next two days as we retraced our steps southward, homeward bound, is beyond the power of my pen or tongue. It must suffice if I say that from dawn until dark each day there was not a moment when the

surroundings did not constitute a charming landscape,
fit for the easel of the most famous artist. At no
time was the ship in a spot the view from which did
not amply repay the trip across the continent.

Nanaimo, on Vancouver's Island, was our next halt,
and here we remained until the ship was re-coaled from
the celebrated mines at this place, a process which occupied an entire afternoon, affording the young men of
our ship an opportunity to be vanquished by the "Nanaimo nine" at base-ball. These mines were recently
the scene of a horrible calamity, resulting from the
careless use of a lamp by a Chinese miner, in which
one hundred and eighty lives were lost—making forty-
one widows and one hundred and forty orphans,—
since which time Chinese labor has been excluded
from the town. The place is decidedly English, prettily located, with beautiful drives, and is said to be the
best hunting and fishing resort on the Pacific Coast.
We took a drive of twelve miles to a trout lake, where,
at a little house in the woods, we were courteously
received by an English gentleman and his wife, who
kindly loaned us their boat and succeeded in doing
every thing for our entertainment excepting to prevail
upon the fish to bite; the few unlucky ones who did
were safely captured. It is not an uncommon thing,
our host told us, to see a dozen deer coming here to
drink in the evening; bear are quite common, and the
whole country is overrun with grouse.

Next morning we debarked once more at Victoria,
where we parted with our friend Mrs. G., who had

EDUCATED ALASKA INDIANS AT HOME.

now reached home, but was willing, she said, to repeat
the trip at any moment. We, of course, took lunch at
the "Poodle Dog," and then drove to 'Squimault, three
or four miles distant, where are the government dock-
yards, and to the boating grounds. It was a lovely
drive, commanding a grand view of the bay and the far-
off Olympic Mountains. It was election day in Victoria,
and this gave the gentlemen of our party an opportunity of studying the new Australian system, which
requires that each voter, before depositing his ballot,
shall shut himself up in a confessional box, and fight
the political campaign out all by himself; and, having
satisfied his conscience, without extraneous interfer-
ence, he is permitted to drop his ticket in the box,
after having marked a big X opposite the names of
the candidates of his choice. Having done this, he immediately tells everybody how he has voted, with the
same volubility that he declared in advance how he was
going to vote. So much for the secrecy of the ballot.
One colored man interested us with the story of his
arrest for illegal voting many years ago, before the
war. It appears there was then a requirement that
all American citizens should be naturalized before
voting. This man had fled to British Columbia from
slavery after the Dred Scott decision had declared
that a slave was *not* a citizen of the United States, and
the Victoria court decided that the requirement did
not apply to him. The gentlemen of our party thought
this quite a *cause célèbre*, and made a note of it. The
trip up Puget Sound was again full of interest, though

THE BOATING GROUNDS AT VICTORIA.

only a repetition, in a mild form, of that exquisite blending of land- and water-scape which we had enjoyed for the past week.

At Port Townsend we rested for a few hours until the custom-house officials had satisfied themselves that we had not smuggled any thing from British Columbia; and here I discovered one or two of my fellow-passengers rather unseasonably clad in fur overcoats, purchased in Victoria. They were evidently wearing them from a sense of *duty* to their government.

We reached the wharf at Tacoma on the morning of Saturday, June 14th, having made the round trip in just twelve days, and I do not hesitate to say that there were no passengers who would not gladly have turned round and faced again to the northward, if their several engagements would have permitted. As for myself, I was bound for the Yosemite, and so little had my Alaska trip fatigued me that I remained in Tacoma for a few hours only, and then started for San Francisco.

These pages I have written at Saratoga Springs, in the midst of the gayest season within my memory. I am surrounded by many dear friends and by acquaintances whom it is a privilege to know. They have given me a most attentive and interested hearing whenever I have taken occasion to speak of my trip to Alaska, and it is a satisfaction to feel that they really want to see my impressions and my photographs published between two covers. What I have seen, you and they may see. Three hundred and fifty dollars cannot be more profitably spent for a summer vacation, and this is more than it costs from New York to the icebergs and back. Think of it! hardly the price of a French costume, a ring, or a bracelet, and yet the memory of such a trip will outlive them all. The pleasure is much enhanced too by the fact that those who are your fellow-passengers are apt to be ladies and gentlemen, by which I mean persons whose good breeding naturally tends to a regard for the comfort of their companions; and among them you will find men and women, young and old, of bright intelligence, who, devoting their time to travel, are full of fact and anecdote—scientists, savants, authors, and artists of renown from all parts of the world.

[*Entre nous*, I have heard of and seen more than one friendship, commencing on an Alaskan trip, which has ripened into mutual pledges "for good or for bad, for better, for worse," and especially of one wealthy and much-travelled Benedict, who was accustomed to congratulate himself that

> " A bachelor
> May thrive, by observation, on a little;
> A single life 's no burthen " ;

but who fell a victim in Alaskan waters to female charms, in furs and ulster, resulting in

> " A contract of eternal bond of love
> Confirme . y mutual joinder of their hands."

and, happily, there are no regrets.]

If you take this trip as I have taken it, you will return home with a theme which will force you to

Lightning Source UK Ltd.
Milton Keynes UK
UKHW010818011218
333087UK00011B/1652/P